HEALTHY START KIDS' COOKBOOK

The Healthy Start Kids' Cookbook: Fun and Healthful Recipes that Kids Can Make Themselves ©1994 edited by Sandra K. Nissenberg, M.S., R.D.

Library of Congress Cataloging-in-Publication Data

Nissenberg, Sandra K., M.S., R.D.

The Healthy Start Kids' Cookbook: Fun and Healthful Recipes that Kids Can Make Themselves / Sandra K. Nissenberg, M.S., R.D.

Includes index
ISBN 1-56561-054-7; $9.95
1. Recipes for children

Research Editor: Patricia Richter
Cover Design: Emerson, Wajdowicz Studios Inc./NYC
Text Design: Nancy Nies, Janet Hogge
Editorial Production Manager: Donna Hoel
Art/Production Manager: Claire Lewis
Production Artist: Janet Hogge
Printed in the United States of America

Published by
CHRONIMED Publishing, Inc.
P.O. Box 47945
Minneapolis, MN 55447-9727

TABLE OF CONTENTS

GETTING STARTED 1

Choosing to eat the healthy stuff. 1

What's in a good meal 2

The food pyramid 2

Learn the pyramid from the bottom up 3

About vitamins and minerals 4

Water 5

How do we measure food 6

Understanding calories 9

Measuring fat, protein, and carbohydrates. 10

How to read labels 10

Eating less fat and sugar 12

My food pyramid` 13

Some secret tips for making food more healthy 16

SAFETY FIRST 16

Getting ready to cook 18

Kitchen tools 18

Words that tell you what to do when you are cooking. 25

Abbreviations—what they mean 28

KITCHEN CLEANUP 30

III

BREAKFAST. 31

Why eat breakfast?. 31

The best kind of breakfast. 31

Fruit always works. 32

RECIPES:

Raspberry Smoothie. 33

Fruit Fling 34

Blender Banana Blitz 35

Fizzy Fruit Slush 36

Bananas on a Stick. 38

Your Own Blender Applesauce. 39

Chilly Cherry Soup 40

No-Time-To-Eat Breakfasts 42

Rice Puff Fluff 43

Icy Grapes to Go 44

Homemade Granola 45

Granola Glaze. 46

Breakfast Granola Bars. 48

On-the-Bus Breakfasts 49

Lazy-Day Choices 49

Creamy Scrambled Eggs. 50

Painted Toast 51

Egg-Citing Surprise. 52

Make-A-Face Breakfast Sandwiches 53

Tangy Taters 54

FUN WITH LUNCHES 57

Why eat lunch? 57

What's the best lunch? 57

No-time-for-lunch lunches 58

Something different 59

RECIPES:

Kids' Quick Chili 60

Tunapple Salad with Orange Dressing 62

Colorful Coleslaw 64

Tossed Super Salad 66

Pocketful of Tuna 67

Cheesy Chicken Sandwiches 68

Pickety Pockety 69

Sunshine Salad 70

Sunny Days Salad 72

Dippity Dilly Vegetable Dip 73

Sweet Potato Chips 74

Cory's Crunchy Crust Pizza 75

Mini Veggie Pizzas 76

Southern Cornbread 78

Sunny Honey Banana Bread 80

Chocolate Chippies 82

Mighty Fine Fudge Brownies 84

AFTER-SCHOOL SNACKS . . . 87

Snacking is good for you 87

First choice—fruits and vegetables 87

RECIPES:

Fruit or Veggie Kabobs 88

Perfect Pops 90

Snowy Fruit Flurry 91

After-School Applesauce 92

Cucumber Circles 94

Rosy Radish Flowers 95

Curling Carrot Cut-Ups 96

Baked Potatoes 97

Tater Toppers 98

Potato Wedgies 100

Katie's Paint Your Pizza 102

Sorry Charlie Sailboats 103

Open-Faced Pizzawich 104

Cinnamon Apples for Four 105

Crunchy Cereal Mix 106

Super Snack Bars 108

YOUR EVENING MEAL . . . 111

What's the best dinner?. 111

How much food do you need to grow?. 111

Planning for big events. 112

RECIPES:

Basic Spaghetti with Meatless Sauce 112

Side-Dish Broiled Meatballs 114

Alphaghetti 116

Easy Lasagna 118

Chicken Nuggets 120

Really Nice Chicken with Rice. 122

Friendly Fowl in Foil Chicken Dinner Bake. 124

Fish in a Flash 126

Creamy Tuna on Toast 128

Chinese Stir-Fry with Shrimp. 130

Potato Salad 132

Baked Tomatoes. 134

Cheesy Green Beans 136

Tossed Salads. 137

Buttermilk Dressing 137

Basic French Dressing 138

Strawberry Dressing 140

Three Fruit Salad 142

Yokota Salad 144

Apple Crisp 146

Wobbly Fruit 148

Aloha Flip 150

EZ Orange Sherbet 152

SPECIAL STUFF 153

Special occasions and baking days 153

Baked goods 153

RECIPES:

Gingerbread Muffin Mix 154

Beetle Muffins 156

Bananarama Muffins 158

Bake-It-Yourself Banana Bread 160

Mighty Fine French Toast 162

Sweet and Chunky Toast Topper 164

French Toast for Friends 166

Perfect Pancakes 168

Shake and Make Pancakes 170

Paint A Pancake 172

There's a Mouse in my House Pancakes 173

Pretzels 174

Tortilla Chips with Homemade Salsa 176

Salsa 178

Let's Try a Pie 180

Purple Moo Moo 182

Icy Pops 183

ACKNOWLEDGMENTS

Special thanks to all the special people who helped with this project . . .

- The Nissenberg Family, who encouraged Mom's hard work

- Stephen Lewis, creative cook and writer

- Claire Lewis, supportive Mom and recipe gatherer

- Katherine (Katie) Richter, super recipe tester

- Cory Scott Richter, chef extraordinaire

- Harry Richter, Katie and Cory's grandpa, who patiently endured the takeover of his house by the young cooks

- The boys and girls of the Minnetonka (MN) Children's Choir Program for ideas and inspiration

- Janet Hogge, graphic artist, who made the book fun

- Jeanne Lutgen, reading specialist, for help with the words

- Jolene Steffer, gifted copy editor and proofreader, who made the message clear

. . . and to all the Moms and Dads, Grandmas and Grandpas, day-care providers, cooks, teachers, custodians, and super grown-ups who work with us in the kitchen.

GETTING STARTED

Choosing to eat healthy stuff

Everybody has a body to take care of. We know that kids should take special care of their bodies because they are so busy—busy growing, busy learning, busy playing. All that busy-ness uses energy. And energy in our bodies comes from the food we eat, just like energy in a car comes from gasoline.

Food is fuel.
When you feel hungry, your body is telling you it needs fuel. That's when you should eat—when you are hungry. It takes your body about 20 minutes to tell you that it has enough fuel, so be sure to eat slowly and stop when you get that full feeling.

We want our bodies to work just right.
We also want to feel well and happy and have plenty of energy to last from breakfast until bedtime. So we need to give our bodies the right fuel throughout the day.

Learning what fuel is right for your body is what this book is all about. There are foods that help your bones and teeth to grow. There are other foods that help your hair and skin stay healthy. Because of your special needs as a kid, you need to know what foods will give you all the energy you need.

What's in a good meal?

Food has been sorted out into groups so we can know how much and what kind of food our bodies need. These groups have names like

**breads, cereals, rice, and pasta
fruits
vegetables
meats, poultry, fish, dry beans, and eggs
milk, yogurt, and cheese**

To help us understand what kind of foods we should eat more of to stay healthy, some grown-ups drew this picture. It is called a "food pyramid."

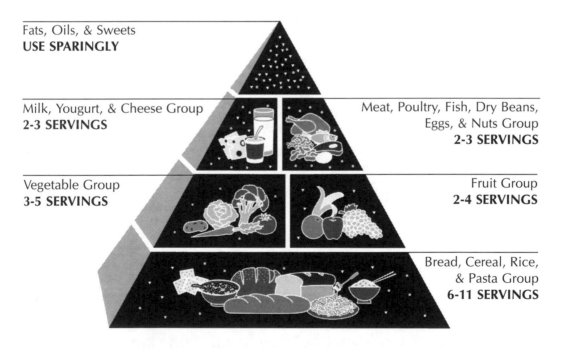

Fats, Oils, & Sweets
USE SPARINGLY

Milk, Yougurt, & Cheese Group
2-3 SERVINGS

Meat, Poultry, Fish, Dry Beans, Eggs, & Nuts Group
2-3 SERVINGS

Vegetable Group
3-5 SERVINGS

Fruit Group
2-4 SERVINGS

Bread, Cereal, Rice, & Pasta Group
6-11 SERVINGS

Every day our bodies need special fuel—called nutrients—from all the different food groups.

There are nutrients that supply calories (food energy). These are protein, carbohydrates, and fats. There are also nutrients that don't have any calories. These are vitamins, minerals, and water. We need a combination of all these nutrients each day.

Learn the pyramid from the bottom up

When you look at the pyramid, you can see we need quite a lot of the **bread, cereal, rice,** and **pasta** group—at least 6 servings every day. These foods give us carbohydrates and lots of energy. Be sure to choose foods from this group that include whole grains like whole-wheat breads and cereals and brown rice.

We need lots of **fruits** and **vegetables**, too—at least 5 servings every day. They give us vitamins and minerals that help our bodies in many different ways.

We need **protein** to make our muscles grow and stay strong. It comes from meat, poultry, fish, eggs, and beans. We don't need very much protein, though, as you can see from the pyramid. Two servings a day is plenty.

Dairy foods include milk, cheese, and yogurt. These foods give us healthy teeth and help our bones grow and stay strong. Remember to drink 2 to 3 glasses of milk every day. The 2% milk and low-fat dairy foods are the best for you.

When we look at the top of the pyramid, we can see we only need a teeny amount of fat and sugar each day. But remember, we do need some. So enjoy your favorites—but not too often and not in place of other healthier foods.

About vitamins and minerals

Vitamins and minerals do many things to keep our bodies strong and healthy. You need to eat foods that contain a lot of vitamins and minerals every day. Some people take vitamin pills, but if you eat healthy foods, you shouldn't need to take the pills.

Many vitamins are named by letters of the alphabet, like vitamin A, vitamin B, vitamin C, and so on. Minerals have strange sounding names like selenium, calcium, and magnesium.

It isn't important to know all about vitamins and minerals, but you do need to know that getting enough of the right vitamins and minerals every day is important for your body. And the best way to get them is by eating the right stuff. If you eat 5 fruits and vegetables a day, along with the right amount of other foods from the food pyramid, you will be getting enough vitamins and minerals.

Water

Water is your body's best friend. As a matter of fact, more than half of your body is made of water. Every single day your body loses 6 to 12 cups of water. So every day you need to put the water back. Try to drink at least 6 cups of water every day.

Some water comes from the food we eat. Fruits and vegetables have lots of water—and so does milk. They are very good for your body.

Water carries fuel to all our cells. Cells are the smallest parts of our bodies, but they do the most work because they make us grow. After the cells take the fuel, the water carries away the leftovers. These are flushed out of the body when you go to the bathroom.

Water is also just like a pillow in some places in our bodies. It makes a soft cushion around our brain and around our lungs and protects them from getting hurt when we stand on our heads or get punched in the chest.

Water has one more really important job. It keeps our bodies at just the right temperature—usually around 98.6°. When you are sick, someone probably checks your temperature. When it is higher than 98.6°, you probably don't feel very well. Then you need to drink even more water to help your body cool down.

Soda pop doesn't help your body the same way water does. So the next time you feel thirsty, skip the soda and have a nice refreshing glass of water.

How do we measure food?

When we were talking about water a while ago, we said to drink 6 CUPS of water each day. A cup is a serving of water.

A cup is also measured in ounces. If you have a measuring cup handy, look at the numbers on it. Usually there is a side that says "Ounces" or "OZ." The line that shows the number 8 is where you stop when you are pouring one cup. Eight ounces is the same as 1 cup.

When we cook, we always use a measuring cup for things that are liquid—like milk and water.

We can use a measuring cup to help us measure servings of other foods, too. A serving of sliced or chopped fruit is usually 1/2 of a cup. A serving of fruit juice is 3/4 of a cup. Look at the measuring cup again, and you will see the other markings. There usually are marks for 1/3 cup, 1/2 cup, 2/3 cup, and 3/4 cup.

When we talk about a serving of fruit, we usually mean a medium-sized fruit. That means not too big and not too small. A medium-sized orange is about the size of a tennis ball—a lot bigger than a ping-pong ball. This is true for apples, too. The next time you go to a grocery store, see if you can spot small, medium, and large fruits.

Tennis ball   **Medium orange**   **Ping pong ball**

A serving of vegetables is measured in a measuring cup, too. A serving of lettuce fills the cup. A serving of cooked corn only fills half the cup. And a serving of vegetable juice, like V8® or tomato juice, is 3/4 of a cup.

A serving of bread, cereal, or starch (those foods at the bottom of the food pyramid) can be 1 slice of bread, 1/2 a cup of cooked rice, or half a bagel.

Fats, oils, and sugar are measured in teaspoons. A teaspoon is only a tiny part of a cup.

Here's a list of serving sizes from each of the food groups on the pyramid.

Breads, Cereals, and Starches—(Eat at least 6 servings every day)

One serving = 1 slice of bread
1/2 cup rice or pasta
3/4 cup cereal
1/2 bagel or English muffin

Fruit—(Eat 2 to 4 servings every day)

One serving = 1/2 cup chopped fruit
3/4 cup fruit juice
1 medium orange, apple, or banana

Vegetables—(Eat 3 to 5 servings every day)

One serving = 1 cup raw leafy vegetables
1/2 cup cooked or raw vegetables
3/4 cup vegetable juice

Meat, Poultry, Fish, Eggs, and Dry Beans—(Eat 2 servings every day)

One serving = 1/2 cup cooked beans
1 egg
2 ounces cooked meat (lean beef, chicken, fish)
2 tablespoons of peanut butter

Milk, Yogurt, and Cheese—(Have 3 servings every day)

One serving = 1 cup milk (2% is best)
1 1/2 ounces cheese
1 cup yogurt

Fats, Oils, and Sugars—(Eat no more than 6 servings every day)

One serving = 1 teaspoon oil, mayonnaise, butter, or margarine
1 teaspoon sugar

Understanding calories

Some grown-ups spend lots of time learning about food so they can teach their kids about it. They gave this study of food a name: Nutrition. Nutrition is studying what's in your food and how much fuel (or energy) is in the food we eat.

Every food serving we eat can be measured in CALORIES. Calories are sort of like gallons of gasoline. We need about 2000 calories every day to make our bodies work properly. If we play more than our friends, we need more calories than they do. If we spend more time sitting in front of the TV (which we shouldn't do) we need fewer calories. So, when we eat an apple (which has about 100 calories), we know that now we only need 2000 take away 100 more calories today. Can you do that subtraction?

Measuring fat, protein, and carbohydrates

Some of the food we eat for fuel contains fat. Fat is measured in 2 ways. One way tells us how many GRAMS of fat there are. (A gram is a measure of how much something weighs. One gram weighs about as much as 1 regular paper clip.) Another way to measure fat is by how many total calories it has. Then you can figure out how much of a food is fat by using a percentage. If half of the calories in something come from fat, the percentage of fat is 50%.

Proteins and carbohydrates are also measured in grams. Adults have learned that measuring the nutrition in food is very important for good health. To help everybody know about nutrition, the facts are marked on the labels of foods we buy at the grocery store.

How to read labels

Labels usually start with the words "Nutrition Facts." A label tells us the serving size we should eat and how many servings are in the package. It also says how many calories are in each serving and how much of your day's total a serving of this food might have.

Labels also tell us the amount of total fat and how much cholesterol (a type of fat), sodium (another word for salt), carbohydrate, and protein are in a food. Next, the labels usually give us a list of ingredients.

Here is a picture of a food label from a box of crackers. See if you can find all the nutrition values for calories, total carbohydrates, protein, and total fat.

Nutrition Facts

Serving Size 5 crackers (15 g)
Servings Per Container About 14

Amount Per Serving

Calories 60   Calories from Fat 0

% Daily Value*

Total Fat 0g	0%
Saturated Fat 0g	0%
Cholesterol 0mg	0%
Sodium 170mg	7%
Total Carbohydrate 12g	4%
Dietary Fiber 1g	3%
Sugars 2g	
Protein 2g	

Vitamin A 0% • Vitamin C 0%

Calcium 2% • Iron 4%

*Percent Daily Values are based on a 2,000 calorie diet. Your daily values may be higher or lower depending on your calorie needs:

	Calories	2,000	2,500
Total Fat	Less than	65g	80g
Sat Fat	Less than	20g	25g
Cholesterol	Less than	300 mg	300mg
Sodium	Less than	2400mg	2400mg
Total Carbohydrate		300g	375g
Dietary Fiber		25g	30g

Learning to read labels is very important for taking care of your body. Remember, you need just the right fuel to keep humming along.

Let's play a little game to see if you can find the right nutrition facts to answer these questions:

1. How many of these crackers can you eat to give your body 60 calories worth of fuel?

2. Sodium is another word for salt. Is there any salt in these crackers?

3. How much fat do you find in a serving of these crackers?

4. How much protein is there?

5. Is there any sugar in these crackers?

Eating less fat and sugar

Remember on the food pyramid how the fats and sugars are on the top. That means that we should only eat a teeny amount of them because they do not give us much good fuel for growing or becoming strong. Did you also notice that the size of a serving of these is measured in teaspoons?

Fats and sugars are measured in teaspoons.

Fruits and vegetables are measured in cups.

There was no fat and only a little bit of sugar found on our cracker label. Some foods have a lot of fat. Foods like bacon and hot dogs have quite a bit of fat, but chicken and fish do not—unless they are fried in lots of fat. Butter and margarine are all fat, but low-fat spreads and Butter Buds® have only a little or none at all. Mayonnaise has a lot of fat, but mustard and ketchup don't.

Too much fat is not good for our bodies. Now is a good time to learn to be careful with fat.

Here's how to figure out how you are doing.

MY FOOD PYRAMID

1. Here's what I ate for breakfast:

Food type _____
(Dairy, Breads, Meats, Fruits, Vegetables)

Serving size _____

Food type _____

Serving size _____

If you had cereal, the label on this packaged food said:

Total fat _____

Total carbohydrates _____

Any sugar? _____

2. Here's what I ate for lunch:

Food type _____

Serving size _____

Food type _____

Serving size _____

Food type _____

Serving size _____

The label on this packaged food said:

Total fat _____

Total carbohydrates _____

Any sugar? _____

Any protein? _____

3. My afternoon snack was:

Food type _____

Serving size _____

The label on this packaged food said:

Total fat _____

Total carbohydrates _____

Any sugar? _____

Any protein? _____

4. For my evening meal, I ate:

Food type _____

Serving size _____

Food type _____

Serving size _____

Food type _____

Serving size _____

Food type _____

Serving size _____

The label on this packaged food said:

Total fat _____

Total carbohydrates _____

Any sugar? _____

Any protein? _____

5. Today I drank milk and water.

Write the number of cups of milk here: _____

Write the number of cups of water here: _____

Remember, not everybody eats just 3 meals and 1 snack a day. If you need more space, copy this chart or take a sheet of paper and write down what you ate. Then fill in the number of servings on your pyramid.

The important thing is to eat when you are hungry, and don't eat when you are not. And, when you eat, try to eat those foods that give your body the best fuel for going and growing.

Some secret tips for making food more healthy

Everybody likes to eat things that taste good, but it is usually the fat and sugar that give those good tastes to our food. Because they aren't good for our bodies, we need to learn what to use instead. Here are some tips:

When you make a sandwich or salad, don't use a lot of mayonnaise or salad dressing. Try low-fat types. They actually taste much the same. Also, watch the cream cheese on your bagel. It's full of fat, too.

When you make popcorn, instead of loading it with melted butter, try it plain or use Butter Buds® or Molly McButter® instead. It will taste the same, but it won't have all that fat that will make your pyramid topple.

Sugar makes foods sweet, and everyone likes sweet things. But try to eat sweet foods that are good for you. Choose fruit, graham crackers, and frozen yogurt instead of candy bars, donuts, or cookies. There is nothing wrong with a dessert after a meal. Just don't eat dessert instead of a meal.

SAFETY FIRST

The kitchen can be a really fun place to be. But remember there are a lot of dangerous things in there! The stove and oven, the toaster oven, and the microwave all make things hot, and they can burn you. Boiling water or steam can burn you, too. Knives are sharp and you could get cut. So rule number 1 in the kitchen is:

1. Always be careful in the kitchen!

Be sure there is an adult in the house whenever you decide to cook something. You need to get permission to use the kitchen and you need to be sure you are allowed to turn on the stove or microwave before you start. So rule number 2 is:

2. Be sure to get permission before you cook!

When you are cooking, you'll want to be sure to protect yourself from hot things, so rule 3 is:

3. Don't wear shirts with long or baggy sleeves and don't let your hair hang down near your face. You need to see what you are doing, and keep clothes and hair away from hot places where they could catch on fire.

Remember that steam burns, and even dishes coming out of the microwave are very hot, so rule 4:

4. Always use hot pads or oven mitts to handle hot pots, pans, and plates.

Knives can be dangerous, so rule 5 is:

5. When you use a knife, pay careful attention to what you are doing.

And rule 6:

6. When you walk with a knife in your hand, keep the sharp end pointed down.

Here's something you might not know. Rule 7:

7. NEVER, EVER use an appliance unless you have permission. NEVER put an appliance that plugs into the wall into the sink to clean it. If the toaster oven falls into the sink, DO NOT REACH IN TO GET IT. CALL FOR HELP.

And finally, rule 8:

8. When you feel unsure or unsafe, call for help.

Look for this flag on the recipe pages. It reminds you to think about the safety rules and ask for help.

Finally, have fun in the kitchen, but take your time and be careful. Keep things neat and clean because cleaner is safer. Pay attention to your cooking from beginning to end, read directions, and be sure to clean up the kitchen when you are finished, so you can cook again.

Getting ready to cook

Before you cook, you need to get ready. That means getting the tools together that you will need. That also means knowing how to do what the recipe tells you to do. And, you'll need to know something about kitchen math so you understand how to measure just the right amounts for cooking up a masterpiece. So, let's go on a tour of the kitchen.

Kitchen tools

The kitchen is filled with neat tools and gadgets. Look at the names and the pictures on the next pages. These are the tools you'll need to use for cooking from this book.

Kitchen tools:

baking pan

blender

casserole dish with cover

cake pan

can opener

chopping knife

colander

**cookie or
baking sheet**

cooling rack

cutting board

egg beater

Dutch oven
(a large pot with a lid)

egg separator

electric mixer

frying pan or skillet

grater

hot pad

loaf pan

measuring cups

measuring spoons

metal spatula

mixing bowl

muffin tin

oven mitt

pancake turner

paring knife

pie plate

rubber spatula

sauce pan with lid

scissors

slotted spoon

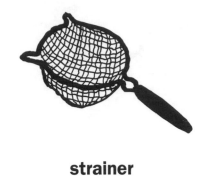

strainer

vegetable peeler

whisk

wooden spoon

24

Words that tell what to do when you are cooking

There are some words that tell us what to do in a recipe. These are called cooking terms and here's a list of what they are and what they mean.

BEAT
This means to use a spoon, a fork, a whisk, or an electric mixer to mix ingredients together, using a fast, circular movement.

BLEND
This means mixing things together until they are smooth or watery. Sometimes it means using an electric blender or mixer.

BOIL
This means to cook water or any liquid on the stove or in the microwave until it bubbles and the bubbles rise to the top of the pot or bowl.

BROWN
This means to cook until the color changes to brown.

CHILL
When you are told to chill something, that means to put it into the refrigerator for at least two hours so it is cold.

CHOP
Chopping is cutting something into small pieces. You can do this using a knife, a food processor, or a blender.

COMBINE
When you combine the parts of a recipe, you toss them together or you place them all in the same bowl.

CUT
Cutting is done with a knife and is done to make something big into smaller pieces.

DICE

When you are asked to dice something, that means to cut it into small square pieces. You need a sharp knife for this, so be careful. The pieces, when diced, are about the same size as dice. Can you see where the name came from?

DRAIN

This means that you need to remove the liquid. You use a colander or strainer to drain something.

GRATE

Find the tool on the Kitchen Tools page called the grater. This is what you use to grate food. Usually you will grate cheese or sometimes carrots. The grater makes the food come out in small pieces or strips.

KNEAD

This means to work the dough with your hands until it is smooth and stretchy. You usually do this on a floured surface. You knead the dough by squeezing, turning, and pressing it down.

MINCE

When the recipe tells you to mince something, that means to cut it or chop it into very small pieces.

MIX

When you mix parts of a recipe, you are putting dry parts, like flour, with creamy parts, like margarine, and liquid parts, like milk or water together. Use a wooden spoon and stir all these parts, called ingredients, so that they are nice and smooth.

SCRAMBLE

When you scramble something, you mix it up really well. To scramble eggs, you stir them while they cook.

SIMMER

When you simmer food, you put it into a saucepan or frying pan on the stove over very low heat and let it bubble a while. Most recipes will tell you how long you need to leave it on the stove.

SPRAY

When you make cookies or bake something in the oven, you may need to spray a cooking oil on the baking pan or the frying pan. There are special spray cans that contain just the right stuff for making sure your cookies don't stick to the cookie sheet.

STIR

When you have combined the parts of a recipe into a bowl or a pan on the stove, you use a large spoon with a long handle to mix them slowly together. Stirring means you move the spoon around and around.

STRAIN

Sometimes a recipe will tell you to use canned fruit, and fruit from cans needs to be strained. When you strain it, it means you pour the fruit from the can into a strainer over a bowl or the kitchen sink. The liquid goes into the bowl and the fruit stays in the strainer. Other canned foods, like vegetables, beans, and pasta need to be strained when they're done cooking.

WASH

You will usually need to wash fresh fruits and vegetables under running water in the kitchen sink to be sure they are clean. When you clean potatoes or carrots, you might want to use a brush or a wash cloth to get all the dirt off.

Abbreviations—
what they mean

Most recipes use what are called abbreviations to tell you how much of each ingredient to put into the dish you are cooking. An abbreviation is a short form of a longer word.

When a recipe calls for you to put in a tablespoon of something, it will be written "Tbsp." A teaspoon is written "tsp." in a recipe. Here's a list of the abbreviations you will find in recipes:

tsp.	=	teaspoon
Tbsp.	=	tablespoon
pkg.	=	package
oz.	=	ounce
med.	=	medium
lb.	=	pound

Here are some other measures you'll use in the kitchen. These are called "equivalents" because they show that one measure is equal to another. This is very helpful when you work in the kitchen.

pinch	=	1/8 teaspoon
3 teaspoons	=	1 tablespoon
4 tablespoons	=	1/4 cup
8 tablespoons	=	1/2 cup
1/4 cup + 1/4 cup	=	1/2 cup
1/2 cup + 1/2 cup	=	1 cup
1 cup	=	8 ounces
1 pound	=	16 ounces

2 cups	=	1 pint	=	16 ounces
2 pints	=	1 quart	=	32 ounces
2 quarts	=	1/2 gallon	=	64 ounces

KITCHEN CLEANUP

There's one more thing you need to know about cooking before we begin. It takes lots of time and lots of tools to make some foods in the kitchen, so cleaning up as you go along is very important.

After you have finished with a bowl or a spoon, put it into the sink. When you have to wait for 5 or 10 minutes for something to bake or cook, use the time to wash the dishes or put them into the dishwasher.

Keeping the kitchen clean as you go along will save lots of mess and confusion later. The grown-ups in your house will like it, too.

Well, we are ready to cook. So grab your apron, and let's head for the kitchen.

START THE DAY OFF RIGHT

Why eat breakfast?

Breakfast is a very important meal for growing bodies. While you were asleep, your body slowed down, like when your car stops at a stop sign. In order to get your body up to speed so you can move along on your day, you need to give it some—you guessed it—fuel. And food is fuel for your body.

There are lots of really yummy things you can make for yourself for breakfast, so you don't ever need to skip breakfast again.

The best kind of breakfast

The best kind of breakfast has just the right fuel to get your day off to a great start. As a matter of fact, many grown-ups believe breakfast is the most important meal of the day. So, don't be a breakfast-skipper.

Try to plan tonight, before you go to bed, for breakfast tomorrow. If you are going to have cereal, get the cereal box out, and get the bowl and spoon ready. (Don't take the milk out of the refrigerator until morning, though.)

Also, you don't want your breakfast to have too much fat or too much sugar. Eating these foods as your first fuel of the day will set you up for an energy let-down by mid-morning. They can make you very sleepy, too, before you even get to lunch.

The best breakfast foods are near the bottom of the food pyramid. Here are some to try.

Fresh fruit or fruit juice.

Low-sugar cereal (like Rice Krispies® or Cheerios®) or a slice of toasted bread or bagel with a non-sugar fruit spread.

And a cup of low-fat milk.

Breakfast never has to be boring! Look through the recipe pages in this book. You'll find lots of creative breakfast ideas that are fun to make and give your body just the right fuel.

Remember, breakfast really is the most important meal of your busy day. If you start your engine without fuel, you can be certain that it will shut down well before lunch. You'll begin to feel tired, cranky, and oooooh sooooo hungry.

Fruit always works

One of the best foods you can eat at breakfast is fruit. You can drink fruit as juice, like orange juice, apple juice, or grape juice. Or you can eat a medium-sized orange, apple, or banana.

Fruit gives your engine a jump-start because it has some natural sugar in it. Besides that, it tastes sweet, so it's yummy. If you have time, you can do very interesting things with fruit. Look at the recipes and then choose some that you can make to have on hand. That way it's easy to get breakfast.

Here are some fruity recipes for you to try.

RASPBERRY SMOOTHIE

Here's a fast shake for the kiddo on the go. You can use low-fat yogurt if you want to, or you can switch the fruit to any kind you like. Put on your chef's thinking cap and come up with something that is all your own.

1 cup	Milk (2%)
2/3 cup	Frozen unsweetened whole raspberries
1/3 cup	Low-fat cottage cheese
1 tsp.	Vanilla extract
1 1/2 tsp.	Sugar
2	Ice cubes
2 to 3 drops	Almond extract

1. Put all the ingredients into the blender.

2. Cover and blend for 45 seconds or until your shake is creamy and smooth.

3. Pour into a tall glass and serve.

Nutrition Information:

One serving	=	1 cup
Calories	=	266
Fat	=	6 gm.
Carbohydrates	=	31 gm.
Protein	=	19 gm.
% Calories from fat	=	23%

Utensils:
Measuring cups, measuring spoons, electric blender, tall glass

Time to
assemble:
3 minutes

Time to blend:
about
45 seconds

Makes
1 serving

FRUIT FLING

You can make this the night before and have it in the refrigerator so it is ready when you are. It's a great way to start a day.

20-oz. can	Pineapple chunks, strained
1 cup	Grapes, washed
2	Bananas, peeled and sliced
1	Red apple, peeled and chopped
1	Orange, peeled and cut into bite-sized pieces
1 tsp.	Lemon juice

1. Find a large bowl with a tight-fitting lid. Pour the pineapple chunks and the grapes into the bowl.

2. Add the sliced bananas, chopped apple, orange pieces, and lemon juice.

3. Put the lid on the bowl. Hold on tightly to the bowl and lid and gently tip the bowl upside down and back, mixing the fruit all up. Tip the bowl 3 more times.

4. Spoon 1 cup of the mixture into a small bowl and eat. If there is any left, you can keep it in your refrigerator in a covered bowl. It will keep for 1 or 2 days.

Time to assemble: 10 minutes

Makes 6 servings

Utensils:
Covered bowl, paring knife, cutting board, can opener, strainer, measuring spoons

Nutrition Information:

One serving	=	1 cup
Calories	=	131
Fat	=	3 gm.
Carbohydrates	=	32 gm.
Protein	=	1 gm.
% Calories from fat	=	2%

BLENDER BANANA BLITZ

This is one to start the night before. Get the first part ready, then add the next part in the morning. Enjoy and off you go!

1 med.	Ripe banana
1 cup	Milk (2%)
1/4 cup	Low-fat vanilla yogurt
1/2 tsp.	Vanilla extract

1. The night before, peel the banana and cut it into 6 chunks. Put all the banana chunks in a plastic sandwich bag or wrap them in plastic wrap and put them into the freezer overnight.

2. The next day, put the banana chunks in the blender. Add the milk, yogurt, and vanilla extract.

3. Blend on low speed until the drink is nice and smooth.

4. When your drink looks thick and creamy, turn off the blender, pour the drink into a glass and enjoy!

Time to assemble: 10 minutes

Makes 1 serving

Nutrition Information:

One serving	=	All of it
Calories	=	211
Fat	=	1 gm.
Carbohydrates	=	39 gm.
Protein	=	12 gm.
% Calories from fat	=	5%

Utensils:
Measuring cup, measuring spoons, plastic bag or wrap, electric blender, drinking glass, table knife

Fizzy Fruit Slush

1 1/2 cups	Orange juice
1 1/2 cups	Water
1 Tbsp.	Honey
6 oz. can	Frozen pineapple juice concentrate
1 med.	Banana
1	Two-liter bottle of lemon-lime soda pop

1. Pour the orange juice, water, and honey into a 2-quart pitcher.

2. Use a can opener to open the pineapple concentrate and add that to the pitcher. Stir until everything is mixed well.

3. Peel a medium banana and use a fork to mash it. Then add it to the pitcher. Mix well.

4. Pour the mixture into a 9- by 5- by 3-inch loaf pan. Cover the pan with foil.

5. Put the loaf pan into the freezer until the mixture is frozen. This should take about 6 hours.

Time to assemble: 25 minutes

Time to freeze: 6 hours

Makes 9 servings of 8 oz. each

To SERVE:

1. Remove the frozen mixture from the freezer and let it stand for about 20 minutes. You'll know it's ready to use when you can scrape the top with a spoon and get some slush.

2. For each serving, scrape off and measure 2/3 cup slush into a tall glass. Then fill the glasses with lemon-lime soda pop.

3. Put any extra slush back into the freezer for another time.

Nutrition Information:

One serving	=	8 oz.
Calories	=	156
Fat	=	0 gm.
Carbohydrates	=	40 gm.
Protein	=	1 gm.
% Calories from fat	=	0

Utensils:
Pitcher, can opener, measuring spoons, measuring cup, 9- by 5- by 3-inch loaf pan, foil paper, fork, spoon, tall glasses

BANANA ON A STICK

Here's a real breakfast treat that is quick, easy, and great on a rushed morning. Make it the night before and it's ready to go.

1 med.	Ripe banana
1	Popsicle® stick
1/8 tsp.	Lemon juice

1. Peel the banana.

2. Carefully insert the popsicle stick into one end of the banana.

3. Sprinkle the banana lightly with the lemon juice. Wrap in plastic wrap and place in freezer overnight.

4. The next morning, remove from freezer and eat on the run.

Nutrition Information:

One serving	=	1 Banana on a stick
Calories	=	100
Fat	=	0 gm.
Carbohydrates	=	27 gm.
Protein	=	1 gm.
% Calories from fat	=	0

Time to assemble:
2 minutes

Makes
1 serving

Utensils:
Popsicle® stick,
measuring spoon,
plastic wrap

YOUR OWN BLENDER APPLESAUCE

Make this ahead of time, put it in a plastic container with a lid, and have it for breakfast or as an after-school snack. It tastes great!

1 small	Apple
1 Tbsp.	Lemon juice
1 tsp.	Sugar
pinch	Ground cinnamon

1. Peel the apple and chop it into little pieces. (Throw the core away.)

2. Combine the apple and lemon juice in the blender. Blend until they are smooth.

3. Stir in the sugar and the cinnamon.

4. Eat immediately or put into covered container and chill in the refrigerator until you are ready to eat.

Time to assemble: 15 minutes

Makes 1 serving

Nutrition Information:

One serving	=	Entire recipe
Calories	=	62
Fat	=	0 gm.
Carbohydrates	=	20 gm.
Protein	=	0 gm.
% Calories from fat	=	0

Utensils:
Knife, cutting board, measuring spoons, electric blender, covered container

CHILLY CHERRY SOUP

Here's one to make the day before and have in the refrigerator for breakfast, snack, or even as a dessert.

20	Large frozen cherries (with no pits in the center)
1/2 cup	Water
1 1/2 tsp.	Sugar
pinch	Cinnamon
1/8 tsp.	Lemon juice
2 Tbsp.	Water (or cherry juice)
1 tsp.	Cornstarch
1/4 cup	Low-fat yogurt, plain

1. In a small pan, combine the cherries, water, sugar, cinnamon, and lemon juice. Bring the mixture to a boil. Lower the heat, cover the pan, and let simmer for 20 minutes.

2. While the cherries are cooking, take a small bowl and combine the 2 tablespoons of water or cherry juice with the cornstarch. Stir until this mixture is nice and smooth and all the cornstarch is dissolved.

3. Carefully remove the lid from the pan and stir in the cornstarch mixture with the cherries. Keep stirring until the whole mixture starts to bubble. Turn down the heat and let the mixture simmer until it becomes thick.

Time to assemble: 45 minutes

Time to cook: about 30 minutes

Makes 2 servings

4. In a heat-proof bowl, stir the yogurt until it is smooth. Add the cherry mixture and stir until everything is nicely mixed. Cover the bowl with plastic wrap, place it in the refrigerator and chill it until it is good and cold.

5. Pour cherry soup into a cup or bowl and enjoy a real treat.

Nutrition Information:

One serving	=	**1/2 cup**
Calories	=	**98**
Fat	=	**1 gm.**
Carbohydrates	=	**19 gm.**
Protein	=	**2 gm.**
% Calories from fat	=	**10%**

Utensils:
Measuring spoons,
measuring cup, small bowl,
long-handled spoon,
covered pan,
heat-proof bowl,
plastic wrap

No-Time-To-Eat Breakfasts

Some mornings you feel in such a hurry, you don't even have time to make your bed before it's off to school. When you feel like you don't have enough time to eat breakfast, it's even more important to have something on hand that you can grab on your way out the door.

So here are some tips:

1. Keep some dry cereal in a plastic bag or container to grab as you leave the house.

2. Of course, grabbing an apple or a banana works really well, too.

3. Perhaps you can take the time to drink a glass of milk, or ask your grownups to have some boxes of milk in the refrigerator for you to take with you.

4. Try the Frozen Banana on a Stick on page 38 for a quick, easy, and nutritious breakfast on the run.

5. A slice of whole wheat toast is a real winning way to start the day. Put some fruit spread on it or drink a glass of your favorite fruit juice with it. For a new taste, spread applesauce on top.

6. A bowl of cereal is always a good choice, and it doesn't take too long to prepare or to eat.

Stay away from those foods that don't contain any real fuel, like donuts and sticky buns. They have too much sugar and they may get your engine started, but they'll let you down quickly. Before the clock strikes 10, you'll feel tired and hungry again.

RICE PUFF FLUFF

Here's a yum-yum cold cereal with a twist. You can substitute Cheerios®, Puffed Rice®, or Rice Chex®.

1/2 cup	Low-fat vanilla yogurt
3/4 cup	Rice Krispies® cereal

1. Put the yogurt in a bowl.

2. Add the Rice Krispies and stir gently.

You can sprinkle a little cinnamon on top, if you like. It's ready to eat.

Time to assemble:
2 minutes

Makes
1 bowl

Nutrition Information:

One serving	=	1 bowl
Calories	=	128
Fat	=	2 gm.
Carbohydrates	=	22 gm.
Protein	=	5 gm.
% Calories from fat	=	15%

Utensils:
Measuring cup,
bowl,
spoon

Fruit is Friendly

Fruit is always a great choice when you are in a hurry. Here's a quick and handy breakfast or snack that you can have in the freezer to grab as you go.

Icy Grapes To Go

1 large bunch   Green grapes

1. Wash the grapes and remove them from the stem. Trim any brown ends.

2. Place the grapes on a flat baking sheet and freeze them for 30 minutes.

3. Move them into a storage jar or individual plastic bags so they are ready when you are.

Nutrition Information:

One serving	=	1/2 cup
Calories	=	35
Fat	=	0 gm.
Carbohydrates	=	9 gm.
Protein	=	0 gm.
% Calories from fat	=	0

Time to assemble: 3 minutes

Time to freeze: 30 minutes

Makes 4 servings

Utensils: Baking sheet, storage jar or plastic bags

HOMEMADE GRANOLA

4 cups	Quick-cooking rolled oats
1/2 cup	Grape-Nuts® cereal
1/4 cup	Sugar
1 cup	Chopped peanuts (buy them chopped)
1/3 cup	Vegetable oil
1/2 cup	Wheat germ
1/2 cup	Raisins

1. Preheat the oven to 350°.

2. Spread the oats on an ungreased baking sheet and heat in the oven for 10 minutes. Then put them into a bowl.

3. Combine the Grape Nuts, sugar, peanuts, and oil and place them on the ungreased baking sheet. Bake for 20 minutes, stirring once to brown evenly. Turn off the oven and let the mixture cool in the oven.

4. Stir the oats, wheat germ, and raisins into the cereal and nuts mixture.

5. Refrigerate in glass jars or plastic containers.

Time to assemble: 20 minutes

Time to bake: About 40 minutes

Makes 6 1/2 cups

Nutrition Information:

One serving	=	1/4 cup
Calories	=	140
Fat	=	7 gm.
Carbohydrates	=	15 gm.
Protein	=	5 gm.
% Calories from fat	=	45%

Utensils:
Measuring cups, baking sheet, bowl, spatula, glass jars or plastic containers

GRANOLA GLAZE

2 cups	Quick-cooking rolled oats
1 cup	Unsweetened shredded coconut
1/2 cup	Wheat germ
1/2 cup	Sunflower seeds
1/4 cup	Slivered almonds
1/2 cup	Margarine
1/4 cup	Honey
1/2 tsp.	Salt
	Vegetable oil cooking spray
2 cups	Raisins

1. Preheat the oven to 350°.

2. In a large bowl, combine oats, coconut, wheat germ, sunflower seeds, and almonds.

3. In a small saucepan, melt together margarine, honey, and salt. When it is all melted, pour this mixture over the oats mixture in the large bowl. Mix it up well with a large spoon.

4. Spread this granola mixture over a baking sheet that you have sprayed with vegetable oil cooking spray.

Utensils:
Large bowl, measuring cups, long handled wooden spoon, baking sheet, small saucepan, hot pads, storage jars

5. Bake for 30 minutes or until the granola looks golden brown. Stir it several times with a long-handled wooden spoon to be sure all sides get browned.

6. Remove granola from the oven, pour it into the large bowl, and mix the raisins in while it is hot.

7. Cool the granola and store it in tightly covered jars or plastic containers.

Nutrition Information:

One serving	=	1/4 cup
Calories	=	128
Fat	=	7 gm.
Carbohydrates	=	16 gm.
Protein	=	3 gm.
% Calories from fat	=	46%

Time to assemble:
20 minutes

Time to bake:
about
30 minutes

Makes
7 cups

BREAKFAST GRANOLA BARS

Make these ahead of time and you've got a portable breakfast.

2 large	Eggs
1/4 tsp.	Salt
1/2 tsp.	Vanilla extract
	Vegetable oil cooking spray
2 1/2 cups	Granola Glaze (from the recipe on page 46)

1. Preheat the oven to 350°.

2. In a medium-sized bowl, combine the eggs, salt, and vanilla. Whip these with a whisk until they are well blended.

3. Add the granola and mix well.

4. Press into an 8-inch square pan sprayed with vegetable oil cooking spray.

5. Bake for 15 to 20 minutes.

6. Remove from oven and cut into 12 bars.

Nutrition Information:

One serving	=	1 bar
Calories	=	119
Fat	=	6 gm.
Carbohydrates	=	13 gm.
Protein	=	4 gm.
% Calories from fat	=	48%

Utensils:
Medium-sized bowl, whisk, measuring cup, measuring spoons, large spoon, 8-inch square baking dish, hot pads

Time to assemble: 20 minutes

Time to bake: about 20 minutes

Makes 12 bars

ON-THE-BUS BREAKFASTS

If you ride the school bus, you'll want a breakfast that not only gets your day off to a good start, but you'll want something "cool" to show the other kids on the bus. Here are some good tips:

Fresh fruit: An apple, a banana, a peach, or a pear,
All are easy and will get you there.

Try dry cereal in a plastic bag:
Crisped rice, very nice;
Big bravos for Cheerios;
Puffed corn in the morn is okay, too;
But granola, homemade is even better for you.

(There's a recipe for homemade granola on page 45.)

Also, breakfast granola bars are great for grabbing on your way.

Or you can try homemade muffins:

There are some that'll make you go bananas (see the recipe on page 158). There are others to freak out your friends (Beetle Muffins, page 156).

All of these will work. Also, if you have a traveling cup, you can take your fruit drinks on board. Don't forget about the frozen grapes. Be creative and invent your own school bus traveling food.

LAZY-DAY CHOICES

Some days, you don't have to get up and rush off to school. On those days, you can cook breakfast for your entire family. Maybe on one of those days you'll want to have pancakes, or you might like to try scrambled eggs. There are recipes in this part of the book that are fun to make and yummy to eat.

CREAMY SCRAMBLED EGGS

For each person at breakfast, use

2	Eggs
1/4 cup	Low-fat cottage cheese
	Vegetable oil cooking spray

1. Break eggs into a bowl. Break the yolks with a fork and stir them up.

2. Add the cottage cheese and stir.

3. Spray the skillet with vegetable oil cooking spray. Turn the burner to medium and heat the empty skillet for 3 minutes.

4. Carefully pour in the eggs and stir while cooking. Eggs are done when they look creamy but not wet. It only takes a few minutes!

Nutrition Information:

One serving	=	3/4 cup
Calories	=	200
Fat	=	11 gm.
Carbohydrates	=	3 gm.
Protein	=	20 gm.
% Calories from fat	=	49%

Time to assemble:
5 minutes

Time to cook:
about
5 minutes

Makes
1 serving

Utensils:
Measuring cup, bowl, fork, spoon, skillet or frying pan

B R E A K F A S T

50

PAINTED TOAST

This one is fun to serve with those creamy scrambled eggs on a special occasion, like your birthday, or just anytime you want to brighten up your breakfast.

2 Tbsp.	Milk, 2%, for each color
2 drops	Food coloring for each color
Slices	Bread, enough for everyone

1. Put milk and food coloring into cups and stir.

2. Using a paint brush, decorate your bread. You can write messages or make patterns. Don't paint the whole piece of bread, just decorate it.

3. Let the bread dry for 10 minutes.

4. Toast the bread. The painted part will be a bright color, and the rest of the bread will be brown!

   Lightly spread some margarine on your toast and enjoy!

**Time to assemble:
5 minutes**

**Drying time:
10 minutes**

**Time to toast:
about
3 minutes**

Nutrition Information:

Each piece of toast has about 70 calories. Check the label on the bread package for the exact number.

**Utensils:
Measuring spoons, cups,
paint brush,
toaster, knife**

EGGS-CITING SURPRISE

Here's a breakfast your parents will enjoy. It's colorful, and if you want to add a zesty taste, put some Mexican salsa on top.

2	Egg whites
1	Whole egg
1 Tbsp.	Water
1 Tbsp.	Onions, chopped
1 Tbsp.	Green pepper, chopped
1/2	Tomato, chopped
	Salt, pepper, spices, to taste
	Vegetable oil cooking spray

1. Use an egg separator to separate yolks and egg whites. In a deep bowl, beat the egg whites, egg, and water together with a fork until the mixture is foamy.

2. Add the chopped vegetables and set the mixture aside.

3. Spray a frying pan with vegetable oil cooking spray. Pour the egg mixture into the frying pan and scramble the mixture over medium heat until eggs are cooked.

These colorful eggs are ready to serve. You can try interesting things like serving this with taco chips, or putting the eggs between two slices of bread to make a sandwich.

**Time to assemble:
15 minutes**

**Time to cook:
about
5 minutes**

**Makes
1 serving**

Nutrition Information:

One serving	=	3/4 cup
Calories	=	127
Fat	=	6 gm.
Carbohydrates	=	6 gm.
Protein	=	13 gm.
% Calories from fat	=	43%

Utensils:
**Egg separator,
measuring spoons,
bowl, fork,
frying pan,
paring knife,
cutting board**

BREAKFAST

MAKE A FACE BREAKFAST SANDWICHES

You can always make a quick egg sandwich by scrambling your eggs and putting them on toast. Here are some other interesting ideas for making faces on your toast for mornings when you have time to be creative.

1 slice	Whole wheat bread, toasted
2 Tbsp.	Applesauce, unsweetened

Make-a-Face Foods
Choose your favorites. We like
banana slices, nuts, blueberries, raisins, and shredded coconut.

1. Toast the bread.

2. Spread 2 tablespoons of applesauce on your toast.

3. Use any of the make-a-face foods to put a face on your toast.

If you have time and want to use cookie cutters to cut out shapes in your toast, you can create camels, clowns, or kitty-cats. Have fun!

Nutrition Information:

One serving	=	1 slice
Calories	=	109
Fat	=	2 gm.
Carbohydrates	=	22 gm.
Protein	=	3 gm.
% Calories from fat	=	17%

Utensils:
Measuring spoons, toaster, knife

Time to assemble: about 15 minutes

Time to toast: about 3 minutes

Make as many slices as you want

TANGY TATERS

This is a side dish that you can have for breakfast, brunch, lunch, or dinner. At breakfast or brunch, serve it with your eggs. If you do not like to eat onions, just leave them out.

2 med.	Potatoes
1/2 small	Onion
1/4 cup	Chicken bouillon
to taste	Salt, pepper, spices
	Vegetable oil cooking spray

1. The night before you want to eat them, poke the potatoes several times with a fork, then bake them for 1 hour in the oven at 350°. Or bake them in the microwave for about 8 minutes, turn them, and bake another 5 minutes. Poke with a fork to be sure they are done. Put the baked potatoes in the refrigerator overnight.

2. Slice the baked potatoes lengthwise, leaving the skin on. Then cut each half crosswise into 1/4-inch half circles.

3. Chop the onion, then combine the onion and potatoes in a bowl. Set it aside.

Time to assemble: 20 minutes

Time to bake: potatoes = 1 hour in oven or 13 minutes in microwave

Makes 2 cups

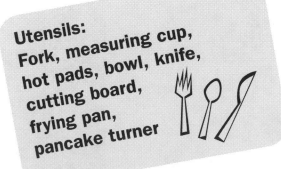

Utensils:
Fork, measuring cup, hot pads, bowl, knife, cutting board, frying pan, pancake turner

4. Spray a nonstick frying pan with vegetable oil cooking spray. Pour in the chicken bouillon.

5. Turn the stove on to medium. Put the potato mixture in the frying pan. Sprinkle the mixture with the seasonings, and cook until the potatoes are golden brown. Turn them often with a pancake turner to be sure they get cooked on all sides.

Nutrition Information:

One serving	=	1 cup
Calories	=	156
Fat	=	trace
Carbohydrates	=	35 gm.
Protein	=	5 gm.
% Calories from fat	=	1%

FUN WITH LUNCHES

Why eat lunch?

Lunch is one of the meals important for filling out your pyramid.

When you are at school, lunch is the time you refuel and get ready for the afternoon. You need to fill your tank with premium food so you're not sleepy the rest of the day.

What's the best lunch?

Remember that all the foods you eat work together to make you grow and help you go, go, go. When trying to figure out what's best for lunch, think about what you had for breakfast. Then add more choices from your pyramid. You also want to be sure you are working toward at least 5-a-day of those fruits and vegetables.

The following pages have some recipes for you to use when you are in charge of lunch. Try them out and have fun.

No-time-for-lunch lunches

Lunch time at school is one of the times you can get together with your friends and, if you have enough time, maybe even go outside for a little while before it's back to class.

Here are some suggestions for lunch-time food on the go:

Fast Food for Lunch Idea #1

Use a plastic container with a lid and fill it with whatever was leftover from dinner last night. Most cooked foods can be eaten cold, and if you liked it yesterday, you'll love it today.

Fast Food for Lunch Idea #2

Take an apple and a slice of whole wheat bread with a small spread of peanut butter. Apples taste especially good with peanut butter, but remember that peanut butter has a lot of fat so you don't want to eat too much of it. That fat is the stuff that topples your pyramid. Buy a container of milk at school, and you've got a well-balanced lunch.

Fast Food for Lunch Idea #3

Fill a plastic container with carrot sticks, celery sticks, and cucumber slices, and crunch, crunch, crunch your lunch. There's a recipe in this chapter for vegetable dip that you can pack in another small plastic container to take, too. Getting your milk at school is a sure way to know that it'll be cold and refreshing.

Fast Food for Lunch Idea #4

Fresh fruit is an excellent choice for school lunch. When you take it to school in its own wrapping you can just peel and eat. Try an apple (eat the peelings), an orange, a banana, a tangerine, some plums, or some grapes. Be adventurous and try new things. You might find you like kiwi fruit or mangoes. Talk to your grown-up about what's available at the grocery store.

And remember, a glass of milk at lunchtime is good fuel for the afternoon.

Something different

When you are not in a rush, there are lots of lunch treats to try that are really fun to make and great to eat. Here are some recipes for you to experiment with. Remember, working in the kitchen is like being a scientist. You need to try things and be ready for a surprise. You might find you like to eat something you've never thought of trying before.

KIDS' QUICK CHILI

1/2 cup	Chopped onion
1 16-oz. can	Kidney beans
1 lb.	Extra lean ground beef
2 Tbsp.	Chili powder
1/2 tsp.	Garlic powder
1/2 tsp.	Black pepper
1 Tbsp.	White vinegar
1 10 3/4-oz. can	Tomato soup
1 soup can	Water

Time to assemble: 15 minutes

Time to cook: 15 minutes

Makes 6 servings

1. Chop onions and set aside.

2. Open the kidney beans and drain them in the colander. Rinse them under cold water and transfer to a bowl.

3. Turn the burner to medium. Heat a large skillet for about one minute. (You want the meat to start cooking as soon as you put it in the skillet.)

4. Add the ground beef and brown.

5. After it's browned, pour the ground beef into the colander and drain. Pat the meat gently with paper towels to soak up some of the grease. Put the meat back into the skillet.

6. Add the rest of the ingredients to the skillet (onions, kidney beans, chili powder, garlic powder, pepper, white vinegar, tomato soup and water).

7. Stir all the ingredients together.

8. Cook over medium heat until it begins to bubble. Turn to low and cook uncovered for 15 minutes. Stir occasionally to keep the chili from burning on the bottom of the pan.

If the chili begins to look thicker than you want it to be, add water, a little bit at a time, until it looks like the chili you like to eat!

Nutrition Information:

One serving	=	2/3 cup
Calories	=	263
Fat	=	10 gm.
Carbohydrates	=	21 gm.
Protein	=	22 gm.
% Calories from fat	=	35%

Utensils:
Colander, knife, measuring cup, cutting board, bowl, paper towel, skillet, measuring spoons, can opener

SALADS

Salads are a great lunch for anytime but especially on days when you want to have a refreshing break from the sunshine.

TUNAPPLE SALAD WITH ORANGE DRESSING

This salad is yummy. You make the dressing first.

Orange Dressing

1/2 cup	Low-fat vanilla yogurt
1/2 tsp.	Orange peel, finely grated
1/2 tsp.	Orange flavored extract

1. Mix all ingredients together in a small bowl.

2. Your dressing is ready. Put it in the refrigerator while you make the salad.

Tunapple Salad

2 cups	Lettuce, washed, dried, and broken into bite-size pieces
1 cup	Red apples, not peeled, but chopped with skin on
6 1/8 oz. can	Water-packed tuna, drained
1	Orange, peeled and sectioned
1/4 cup	Orange Dressing (above)

Utensils:
Knife, measuring spoons, grater, measuring cup, can opener, colander, stirring spoon, bowls

1. Toss lettuce, apples, tuna, and orange together in a large bowl.

2. Serve the salad on salad plates and pour the dressing over each serving.

Nutrition Information for dressing:

One serving	=	1 Tbsp.
Calories	=	13
Fat	=	trace
Carbohydrates	=	2 gm.
Protein	=	1 gm.
% Calories from fat	=	13%

Nutrition Information for salad:

One serving	=	1 cup salad
Calories	=	80
Fat	=	1 gm.
Carbohydrates	=	9 gm.
Protein	=	10 gm.
% Calories from fat	=	6%

Time to assemble: 15 minutes

Makes 4 servings

COLORFUL COLESLAW

Maybe you think you don't like cabbage. Here's a really tasty treat. If you make this, your whole family will eat it all up.

2 cups	Shredded carrots (about 4 to 6 medium carrots)
2 cups	Shredded red cabbage (about 1 small head)
1/4 tsp.	Orange peel
1 6-oz. container	Low-fat orange or lemon yogurt
1/8 tsp.	Salt
6 Tbsp.	Unsalted, dry-roasted peanuts
1/2 cup	Mandarin orange sections in light syrup, drained

1. Place the shredded carrots and cabbage in a medium-sized bowl. Use your hands (be sure they are clean) to mix these together thoroughly. (You'll want to wash your hands again after you do this.)

2. To get the orange peel, use a grater and rub an orange against the smallest holes to get very tiny pieces of orange peeling. Measure 1/4 teaspoon of the grated orange rind into a small bowl.

Nutrition Information:

One serving	=	1/2 cup
Calories	=	139
Fat	=	6 gm.
Carbohydrates	=	18 gm.
Protein	=	6 gm.
% Calories from fat	=	36%

3. Add the yogurt and the salt to the bowl with the orange rind. Stir these together very well, using a wooden spoon.

4. Add the yogurt mixture to the carrot-cabbage mixture and stir very well to mix thoroughly.

5. Add the peanuts. Stir until everything is well mixed.

6. Drain the mandarin orange sections in a colander. Measure out 1/2 cup and add these to the bowl. Gently mix the orange sections in using a rubber spatula. Be careful because you don't want the orange pieces to break.

Your slaw-style salad is ready to serve, or you can make this ahead of time and put it in the refrigerator. Use plastic wrap to cover the bowl.

Time to assemble: 25 minutes

Makes 5 servings

Utensils:
Measuring cups, medium bowl, grater, small bowl, measuring spoons, wooden spoon, can opener, colander, rubber spatula, plastic wrap

TOSSED SUPER SALAD

This is a salad you can eat every day. It is tasty and filled with things that are great for your body. You can make enough to serve the whole family and then save some for dinner or lunch tomorrow.

4 cups	Lettuce, washed, dried, and torn into bite-size pieces
3	Medium carrots, cut into rounds
2	Stalks celery, cut into thin slices
2	Ripe medium tomatoes, washed, cut into small wedges

1. Prepare all the ingredients and toss them together in a large bowl.

2. Serve, or cover with plastic wrap and refrigerate until you are hungry.

You can use any salad dressing on this basic salad, and you can add all kinds of good things to it to make it just the way you like it. Some kids like to add bean sprouts and different kinds of lettuce. Other kids want more crunch, and they add apple chunks or nuts.

Time to assemble: 20 minutes

Makes 4 servings

Here's a tip about salad dressings. If you want to take good care of your body, you can mix 1 teaspoon of any creamy salad dressing with 1 tablespoon of nonfat plain yogurt. That way you get all the dressing you need but only a little fat.

Nutrition Information:

One serving	=	1 cup
Calories	=	47
Fat	=	trace
Carbohydrates	=	10 gm.
Protein	=	2 gm.
% Calories from fat	=	8%

Utensils:
Knife, cutting board, salad bowl, plastic wrap

SANDWICHES

Sandwiches are a great lunch. They can be made to go, or you can take your time and make them fancy for fun. Here are some of the sandwiches the kids at our place like.

POCKETFUL OF TUNA

Alfalfa sprouts are terrific with tuna. Try it! If you want to experiment with the recipe, try using grated carrots or chopped apple instead of the water chestnuts.

1 6 1/8-oz. can	Tuna, packed in water
1/2 cup	Celery, chopped
1/2 cup	Water chestnuts, drained and chopped
1 Tbsp.	Onion, finely chopped
2 Tbsp.	Light mayonnaise
1 cup	Alfalfa sprouts
2	Pita pocket breads, each cut in half

Time to assemble: 10 minutes

Makes 4 servings

1. Use the colander over the sink to drain the liquid from the tuna. Flake the tuna into a medium-sized bowl.

2. Chop the celery, water chestnuts, and onion. Add them to the tuna.

3. Add mayonnaise and stir to mix.

4. Put tuna mixture and alfalfa sprouts into the pita pocket.

Nutrition Information:

One serving	=	1 pocket
Calories	=	147
Fat	=	1 gm.
Carbohydrates	=	21 gm.
Protein	=	13 gm.
% Calories from fat	=	5%

Utensils:
Colander, knife, cutting board, measuring cups, measuring spoons, spoon, bowl, can opener

CHEESY CHICKEN SANDWICHES

Here's one to make you cluck.

3 Tbsp.	Diced, cooked chicken
2 tsp.	Light mayonnaise
1	Small dill pickle, chopped (optional)
1 Tbsp.	Low-fat mozzarella cheese, shredded
2 slices	Bread
2	Lettuce leaves

1. Mix together diced chicken, mayonnaise, pickles, and cheese.

2. Spread on one slice of bread.

3. Top with lettuce.

4. Close the sandwich with the other slice of bread. Chow down and enjoy.

Time to
assemble:
10 minutes

Makes
1 serving

Nutrition Information:

One serving	=	1 sandwich
Calories	=	248
Fat	=	8 gm.
Carbohydrates	=	29 gm.
Protein	=	18 gm.
% Calories from fat	=	29%

Utensils:
Knife, cutting board,
measuring spoons,
small bowl

L U N C H E S

PICKETY POCKETY

Pita bread is fun to eat. It tastes great and you can stuff it with anything you like. Here's a sampling of some of the different kinds of sandwiches you can make.

> 1   Pita pocket bread

Choose from these fillings:
—Sprouts or lettuce

—Chunks of cooked chicken or turkey

—Chopped celery, apples, tomatoes, cucumbers, or mushrooms

—Canned garbanzo beans or kidney beans, cooked and chilled

—Grated cheese

—Cottage cheese and crushed pineapple

—Canned low-fat salsa and refried beans

Time to assemble: 5 minutes

Makes 2 servings

1. Pick the filling you want, prepare it, and set it aside.

2. Cut your pita bread in half and open the pocket.

3. Stuff the pocket with your choice of fillings.

You may want to use a little light mayonnaise to keep your sandwich moist, since pocket bread is a little dry.

Nutrition Information:

One serving	**=**	**1/2 pita, stuffed with lettuce, chicken, celery, and tomatoes**
Calories	**=**	**135**
Fat	**=**	**3 gm.**
Carbohydrates	**=**	**18 gm.**
Protein	**=**	**11 gm.**
% Calories from fat	**=**	**22%**

**Utensils:
Knife, cutting board, spoon, small bowl**

FRUIT FOR LUNCH

Fruit is great for breakfast or lunch, or as an afternoon snack. Fruit salad is fine any old time. Try these refreshing fruity recipes.

SUNSHINE SALAD

You can eat this salad just as it is for your lunch, or add some dry-roasted nuts to it to give it a crunch. You can also serve it as a side dish or even as a dessert topped with some whipped topping.

1 21-ounce can	Peach pie filling
1	Medium orange
1/2	Large red Delicious apple
1 cup	Cantaloupe chunks
1 cup	Seedless green grapes, washed
1/2 cup	Seedless red grapes, washed
1	Medium banana

1. Empty the can of peach pie filling into a bowl. Scrape the inside of the can with a spatula to be sure you get all of it.

2. Carefully peel an orange and, using the cutting board, cut the orange carefully in half the long way. Then slice the orange thinly into slices. Put the orange slices into the bowl with the peach pie filling.

3. Wash the half apple and cut it into 1/2-inch thick slices lengthwise. Remove the seeds and the core. Cut each slice into triangles so the red skin is on the bottom of each triangle.

**Time to assemble:
20 minutes**

**Time to refrigerate:
2 hours**

**Makes
5 servings**

4. Cut the cantaloupe into chunks.

5. Add the apple slices, cantaloupe chunks, and grapes to the pie filling.

6. Peel the banana and cut it into slices. Then add it to the bowl.

7. Using a rubber spatula, gently mix all the ingredients.

8. Cover the bowl tightly with plastic wrap and refrigerate for 2 hours before serving.

Nutrition Information:

One serving	=	1 cup
Calories	=	240
Fat	=	0 gm.
Carbohydrates	=	62 gm.
Protein	=	2 gm.
% Calories from fat	=	0

Utensils:
Can opener, sharp knife, cutting board, bowl, spatula, plastic wrap, measuring cups

SUNNY DAYS SALAD

1	Orange
1	Red apple
2	Lettuce leaves
2 Tbsp.	Crushed pineapple, drained

1. Peel and separate orange into segments. Set aside.

2. Core unpeeled apple and slice into wedges. Set aside.

3. Lay a lettuce leaf on a salad plate. Then alternate orange segments and apple wedges on the lettuce leaf to form a sunburst.

4. Put a spoonful of crushed pineapple in the center of the sunburst. Serve.

Nutrition Information:

One serving	=	1/2 recipe
Calories	=	87
Fat	=	0 gm.
Carbohydrates	=	21 gm.
Protein	=	1 gm.
% Calories from fat	=	0

Utensils:
Sharp knife, cutting board, can opener, salad plates, measuring spoon

Time to assemble: 10 minutes

Makes 2 servings

DIPPITY DILLY VEGETABLE DIP

When you want to take a dip to school with your veggie lunch, here's a recipe that is a dilly:

2/3 cup	Low-fat cottage cheese
1/3 cup	Plain low-fat yogurt
1 tsp.	Lemon juice
1 tsp.	Dill seed
1 tsp.	Minced dried onion

1. Blend the cottage cheese, yogurt, lemon juice, dill seed, and onion in the blender on high speed until it is smooth.

2. Once the mixture is smooth, use a rubber spatula and pour the dip into a bowl.

3. Your dip is ready to serve, or put into a plastic container with a lid and store in your refrigerator to take to school with your container of dipping vegetables.

Time to assemble: 10 minutes

Makes 16 servings

Nutrition Information:

One serving	=	1 tablespoon
Calories	=	10
Fat	=	trace
Carbohydrates	=	1 gm.
Protein	=	1 gm.
% Calories from fat	=	trace

Utensils: Measuring cup, measuring spoons, electric blender, spatula, bowl

SWEET POTATO CHIPS

Maybe you like to have some chips at lunchtime. These aren't the crunchy kind, but you'll love their sweet taste.

2   Medium sweet potatoes
     Vegetable oil cooking spray

1. Heat the oven to 450°.

2. Scrub the sweet potatoes and cut them into thin, even slices, like potato chips.

3. Spray a cookie sheet with vegetable oil cooking spray. Put the sweet potato slices on the cookie sheet in a single layer.

4. Bake for 10 to 12 minutes. (If you cut your slices thin, they only need 10 minutes; if they are a little thicker, 12 minutes.)

BE CAREFUL WHEN YOU TAKE THESE OUT OF THE OVEN! The cookie sheet will be very hot. Use hot pads and a pancake turner to remove the chips from the cookie sheet onto a paper towel to cool.

Nutrition Information:

One serving	=	1/2 cup
Calories	=	47
Fat	=	0 gm.
Carbohydrates	=	11 gm.
Protein	=	1 gm.
% Calories from fat	=	0

Time to assemble:
5 minutes

Time to bake:
10 to 12 minutes

Makes
5 servings

Utensils:
Knife, cutting board, cookie sheet, hot pads, pancake turner, paper towel

CORY'S CRUNCHY CRUST PIZZA

Pita bread makes great individual pizzas. This is one of our test chef's favorites. You can make this for one person in your toaster oven. Or make one for each person using the big oven as this recipe shows.

1	Pita pocket bread
1/2 cup	Spaghetti or pizza sauce (from a jar like Healthy Choice®)
2 tsp.	Parmesan cheese, grated
1/3 cup	Low-fat mozzarella cheese, shredded

Time to assemble: 5 minutes

Time to bake: 10 to 15 minutes

Makes 2 servings

1. Preheat the oven to 425°.

2. For the crispy crust, carefully cut the pitas open the long way so you have a round top and a round bottom. Put the rounds in the toaster oven on "toast" for about 2 minutes. Be careful when you take them out because they will be hot and slightly toasted.

3. Lay the pocket bread for each pizza on a cookie sheet.

4. Top each pita with the sauce, Parmesan cheese, and mozzarella cheese.

5. Bake for 10 to 15 minutes. They are done when the cheese melts and begins to brown and bubble.

Nutrition Information:

One serving	=	1 pizza
Calories	=	166
Fat	=	5 gm.
Carbohydrates	=	22 gm.
Protein	=	5 gm.
% Calories from fat	=	24%

Utensils:
Sharp knife, measuring cup, measuring spoons, grater, cookie sheet, hot pads

MINI VEGGIE PIZZAS

Here's another great pizza to make for lunch or as a snack. Use your favorite fresh vegetables as toppers!

8	English Muffins, split in half
8 oz.	Spaghetti sauce (recipe on page 112)
4	Scallions, sliced thin
1	Green pepper, chopped fine
8	Mushrooms, thinly sliced
4 oz.	Low-fat mozzarella cheese, shredded
	Vegetable oil cooking spray

1. Preheat the broiler. (Get a grown-up to help you with this, since this is the hottest kind of oven.)

2. Spray a baking sheet with vegetable oil cooking spray and place the muffin halves on it.

3. Place the baking sheet with the muffin halves into the broiler for 5 minutes.

Nutrition Information:

One serving	=	2 muffin half pizzas
Calories	=	216
Fat	=	4 gm.
Carbohydrates	=	34 gm.
Protein	=	9 gm.
% Calories from fat	=	17%

4. Remove the baking sheet (be sure to use hot pads) and top the muffins with sauce, scallions, chopped pepper, sliced mushrooms, and shredded cheese. BE VERY CAREFUL. The baking pan is very, very hot! Ask for grown-up help.

5. Put the baking sheet back into the broiler for 7 to 10 minutes more, or until the cheese is well melted.

Carefully remove the baking sheet from the boiler and let it cool for 1 minute before removing the pizzas.

Utensils:
Baking sheet,
knife, cutting board,
spoons, hot pads

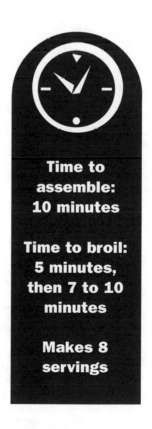

Time to assemble: 10 minutes

Time to broil: 5 minutes, then 7 to 10 minutes

Makes 8 servings

SOUTHERN CORNBREAD

This cornbread is the old fashioned Southern kind and tastes better when it is served hot, without butter or margarine.

2 Tbsp.	Vegetable oil
1	Egg
2 cups	Buttermilk
1/2 cup	Corn, fresh, canned or thawed
1 3/4 cups	Yellow cornmeal
1 tsp.	Salt
1 tsp.	Baking soda

1. Preheat the oven to 450°.

2. Put the vegetable oil in a 9- by 13-inch glass pan. Put the pan of vegetable oil in the oven for 10 minutes.

3. In a medium bowl, stir up the egg. Add the buttermilk and stir well.

4. Stir in the corn.

5. In a small bowl, mix the cornmeal, salt, and baking soda. Be sure to get all the lumps out of the soda.

Nutrition Information:

One serving	=	1 square
Calories	=	122
Fat	=	3 gm.
Carbohydrates	=	19 gm.
Protein	=	4 gm.
% Calories from fat	=	22%

6. When the timer goes off, add the cornmeal mixture to the buttermilk bowl, and stir until all the cornmeal is wet.

7. Carefully remove the pan of hot oil from the oven. Put it on top of the stove. Be sure to use hot pads. The glass pan will be very hot!

8. Pour the cornmeal mixture into the hot pan. It will start to sizzle.

9. Put the pan back in the oven and bake for 25 to 30 minutes.

10. When the cornbread is light brown, remove it from the oven and cut it into 12 pieces.

Time to prepare: 15 minutes

Time to bake: 25 to 30 minutes

Makes 12 servings

Utensils:
Measuring cups, measuring spoons, 9- by 13-inch glass baking pan, medium bowl, small bowl, wooden spoon, hot pads

SUNNY HONEY BANANA BREAD

This is a really yummy banana bread with sunflower seeds. If you don't like them, leave them out and the bread is still a treat to eat.

3	Medium ripe bananas
1/4 cup	Margarine
1/4 cup	Honey
1 Tbsp.	Orange juice concentrate, unsweetened
1 1/2 cups	Whole wheat flour
1 tsp.	Baking soda
1/4 tsp.	Salt
1 tsp.	Vanilla extract
1/2 cup	Sunflower seeds
	Vegetable oil cooking spray

1. Preheat the oven to 350°.

2. Peel the bananas. Put them in a medium bowl, and mash them with a fork.

3. Melt the margarine in a saucepan.

4. Stir in the melted margarine, honey, and orange juice concentrate.

5. In a separate bowl, stir together flour, soda, and salt. Add this mixture to the bananas.

Utensils:
Measuring cups, measuring spoons, 2 bowls, saucepan fork, mixing spoon, 9- by 5-inch loaf pan, hot pads

6. Add the vanilla and sunflower seeds. Mix well.

7. Spray a 9- by 5-inch loaf pan with vegetable oil cooking spray and pour batter into it.

8. Bake at for 55 to 60 minutes.

9. Remove the pan from the oven. Remove the bread from the pan and cool before slicing.

Time to prepare: 15 minutes

Time to bake: 55 to 60 minutes

Makes 1 loaf or 16 slices

Nutrition Information:

One serving	=	1 slice
Calories	=	139
Fat	=	6 gm.
Carbohydrates	=	19 gm.
Protein	=	4 gm.
% Calories from fat	=	39%

And for dessert:

It's always special to have a dessert in your lunch box. Here are two recipes that you can make with only a little help from the grown-up at your house and can easily pack in your lunch box.

CHOCOLATE CHIPPIES

2 1/4 cups	Flour
1 tsp.	Baking soda
1 tsp.	Salt
1/2 cup	Margarine
1/2 cup	Nonfat cream cheese or fat-free ricotta
1/2 cup	Sugar
3/4 cup	Brown sugar, packed
1 1/2 tsp.	Vanilla extract
1/2 tsp.	Butter flavor extract
1	Egg
1	Egg white
1 cup	Chocolate chips, regular or miniature

1. Preheat the oven to 375°.

2. In a small bowl, combine the flour, baking soda, and salt. Set this bowl aside.

Nutrition Information:

One serving	=	1 cookie
Calories	=	138
Fat	=	6 gm.
Carbohydrates	=	20 gm.
Protein	=	2 gm.
% Calories from fat	=	39%

3. In a large bowl, blend the margarine with the cream cheese. Add the sugar, brown sugar, vanilla, and butter extract. Beat this with an electric beater until the mixture is creamy.

4. Beat in the egg and egg white.

5. Slowly add the flour mixture.

6. Stir in the chocolate chips.

7. Use the measuring tablespoon, scoop out some cookie mix, and drop the tablespoonful onto an ungreased cookie sheet.

8. If you like your cookies soft and chewy, bake them for 7 or 8 minutes. If you like them dry, bake one minute longer.

Time to assemble: 20 minutes

Time to bake: 7 to 9 minutes

Makes 30 large cookies

Utensils:
Mixing bowls, egg separator, measuring cups, measuring spoons, electric mixer, mixing spoon, cookie sheets, hot pads

MIGHTY FINE FUDGE BROWNIES

1/2 cup	Margarine
1/2 cup	Nonfat or light sour cream
1 cup and 2 Tbsp.	Cocoa
2	Eggs
3	Egg whites
1 2/3 cups	Sugar
1 tsp.	Vanilla extract
1/2 cup	All-purpose flour
	Vegetable oil cooking spray

1. Preheat the oven to 300°.

2. Spray quite a bit of vegetable oil cooking spray on a 9- by 9-inch baking pan.

3. Melt the margarine in a saucepan.

4. Mix sour cream and cocoa with the melted margarine over low heat on the stove. Stir until the mixture is smooth, then set aside on a trivet or hot pad. (Be sure to turn the burner off on the stove.)

5. In a mixing bowl, beat the eggs and egg whites with an electric mixer until they are light yellow in color. (This takes about 5 minutes.)

Nutrition Information:

One serving	=	1 brownie
Calories	=	174
Fat	=	7 gm.
Carbohydrates	=	25 gm.
Protein	=	3 gm.
% Calories from fat	=	39%

6. Add the sugar and mix on low speed until all the ingredients are combined.

7. Add the vanilla and cocoa mixture and mix again until smooth.

8. Mix in the flour and pour the batter into the baking pan.

Note:
If you like extra chocolate, you can add chocolate chips to the top of the batter just before you put it in to bake.

9. Bake on the center rack of the oven about 45 minutes, or until a toothpick inserted in the center comes out clean. BE CAREFUL! The pan is hot. Use hot pads and set the pan down where it can cool safely.

Let these fudgy brownies cool before you cut them for eating.

Utensils:
Mixing bowls, egg separator,
saucepan, measuring cups,
measuring spoons, electric mixer,
9- by 9-inch baking pan,
hot pads, toothpick

**Time to assemble:
20 minutes**

**Time to bake:
45 minutes**

Makes 16 brownies

AFTER-SCHOOL SNACKS

Snacking is good for you!

The best time to eat is when you are hungry. Then eat just enough so you feel comfortable. When you get home from school, you probably feel ready for a snack. The next pages are full of ideas for healthy snacking.

First choice—
fruits and vegetables

When it comes to snacks, it's hard to beat fruits and vegetables for being crunchy and fun to eat. But your fruits and veggie choices don't have to be dull.

Try some of these for fun:

FRUIT OR VEGGIE KABOBS

Take your favorite fruits or vegetables, and cut them into squares that are at least 1inch on each side. Take a wooden skewer stick and put the pieces on, alternating. Here's how:

For a fruit kabob:

1/2	Red apple
1 can	Pineapple chunks
1 bunch	Red grapes
1 bunch	Green grapes
1	Small banana

1. Cut the apple into 1-inch wedges. Leave the skin on to make your kabob colorful.

2. Drain a can of pineapple chunks in a colander over the sink.

3. Wash the grapes and remove them from the stem.

4. Peel the banana and slice it into 1/4-inch thick rounds.

5. Now take the skewer stick and first put on an apple wedge, then add a pineapple chunk. Next put on a red grape, then a banana, and then a green grape.

Keep doing this until your kabob stick is covered end-to-end with fruit. Serve these kabobs on the sticks and watch how everyone enjoys them.

Time to prepare: 10 minutes

1 Kabob = 1 Serving

For a vegetable kabob:

1 stalk	Celery
1	Small carrot
12	Small cherry tomatoes
1	Small green pepper

1. Wash all the vegetables and pat them dry with paper towels.

2. Cut the celery into 1/2-inch pieces.

3. Cut the carrots into 1/4-inch rounds.

4. Clean the green pepper, being sure to get out all the seeds. Cut the pepper into pieces about 3/4-inch square.

5. Take the kabob stick and place a celery piece on the end.

6. Add a piece of carrot, a tomato, a green pepper square, another celery, another carrot, another tomato, and so on until the kabob stick is full.

This is a good snack to use with the Dippity Dilly Vegetable Dip on page 73.

Utensils:
Cutting board and knife, colander, can opener, paper towels, kabob skewers or sticks

Nutrition Information:

Depends on which fruits and vegetables you choose, but you can be sure the fuel value will be high and the sugar and fat will be low.

PERFECT POPS

This fruity treat is easy to make and delicious to eat. These pops are perfect after a long day at school or a hard afternoon of play. Make them the night before.

2 cups	Orange juice
1/2 cup	Low-fat vanilla yogurt

1. Pour the orange juice into the blender and add the yogurt.

2. Put the top on the blender and blend at high speed for about 1 minute.

3. Pour the mixture into 6 small paper cups. Put a Popsicle® stick or a plastic spoon into each cup.

4. Put the cups into the freezer overnight.

5. Hold the cup under hot water to loosen the pop from the cup.

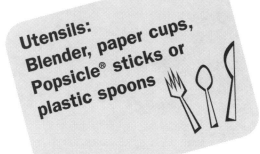

Utensils:
Blender, paper cups, Popsicle® sticks or plastic spoons

Time to prepare: 3 minutes

Time to freeze: overnight

Makes 6 servings

Nutrition Information:

One serving	=	1 pop
Calories	=	47
Fat	=	1 gm.
Carbohydrates	=	10 gm.
Protein	=	1 gm.
% Calories from fat	=	13%

SNOWY FRUIT FLURRY

If you like ice cream, you'll love this.

1 cup	Milk, 2%
2 cups	Peaches, sliced, canned or fresh
	OR
2 cups	Strawberries
2 tsp.	Sugar

1. Freeze the milk in ice-cube trays.

2. When you're ready to eat this, put the frozen milk and the fruit in the blender.

3. Blend on high speed until the fruit and milk are thoroughly mixed.

4. Pour the mixture into serving dishes. If you have any left over, store it in the freezer.

Time to prepare:
3 minutes

Makes
8 servings

Nutrition Information:

One serving	=	1/4 cup
Calories	=	33
Fat	=	trace
Carbohydrates	=	8 gm.
Protein	=	1 gm.
% Calories from fat	=	trace

Utensils:
Blender,
spatula

AFTER-SCHOOL APPLESAUCE

Make this one on the weekends, keep it in the refrigerator, and you can have it right away when you get home from school or sports.

4	Apples
1 cup	Water
3 Tbsp.	Honey
1/4 tsp.	Cinnamon
1/8 tsp.	Nutmeg

1. Wash, peel, and cut up the apples.

2. Put the apples and water in a medium saucepan.

3. Bring water to a boil.

4. Cover the pan and turn the heat down to medium-low. Cook for 10 minutes.

5. Uncover the pan and cook over medium heat for 5 more minutes. BE CAREFUL! THERE WILL BE SOME STEAM COMING UP WHEN YOU TAKE THE LID OFF.

Utensils:
Knife, cutting board, medium saucepan, measuring cup, measuring spoons, electric blender, hot pad

SNACKS

6. Remove the pan from the stove and put it on a hot pad or trivet to cool for a few minutes.

7. Pour the contents of the pan into the blender and blend until the mixture is nice and smooth (about 2 minutes). Add the honey and spices and blend for 10 seconds more.

Nutrition Information:

One serving	=	1/2 cup
Calories	=	87
Fat	=	1 gm.
Carbohydrates	=	23 gm.
Protein	=	0 gm.
% Calories from fat	=	4%

Time to assemble: 15 minutes

Time to cook: 15 minutes

Makes 6 servings

CUCUMBER CIRCLES

1 Cold cucumber

1. Peel the cucumber completely. Then pull the tines of a fork down the cucumber lengthwise. Repeat this until the entire cucumber is marked with little ridges from the fork.

2. Slice the cucumber crossways into rounds.

The cucumber slices are ready to eat.

Maybe you like veggie dips. Try the Dippity Dilly Vegetable Dip recipe on page 73.

Nutrition Information:

One serving	=	1 cucumber
Calories	=	30
Fat	=	trace
Carbohydrates	=	6 gm.
Protein	=	trace
% Calories from fat	=	trace

Time to prepare: 3 minutes

Makes 1 serving

Utensils:
Vegetable peeler, cutting board, knife, fork

ROSY RADISH FLOWERS

5   Radishes

1. Wash and cut off the top of the radishes so that some of the white from the inside is showing.

2. Make 3 evenly spaced diagonal cuts the long way, near the edge of each radish. Be careful not to cut all the way through the radish.

3. Chill the radishes in ice water until they are crisp. (About 7 minutes.)

When the radishes come out of the ice water, the tops where you cut will look like flowers.

Serve, eat, and enjoy.

Utensils:
Knife,
cutting
board,
bowl

Time to
prepare:
3 minutes

Time to chill:
about 7
minutes

Makes
1 serving

Nutrition Information:

One serving	=	5 radishes
Calories	=	20
Fat	=	trace
Carbohydrates	=	5 gm.
Protein	=	trace
% Calories from fat	=	trace

CURLY CARROT CUT-UPS

These are fun for yourself or as a treat for your friends. They look kind of fancy and are fun to dip and pop into your mouth.

1   Carrot

1. Peel the carrot.

2. Slice the carrot almost as thin as a piece of paper using the vegetable peeler.

3. Roll each strip up into a curl and put in a toothpick to hold it.

4. Put the carrot curl-ups into ice water in a bowl and let stand until the carrots stay curled when the toothpicks are removed.

Time to prepare: 5 minutes

Makes 1 serving

Utensils: Vegetable peeler, bowl, toothpicks

Nutrition Information:

One serving	=	1 carrot
Calories	=	60
Fat	=	trace
Carbohydrates	=	14 gm.
Protein	=	2 gm.
% Calories from fat	=	trace

BAKED POTATOES

Did you know that baked potatoes make an excellent snack? They do, so if you love potatoes, here are some ideas.

4   Medium baking potatoes

1. Turn on the oven to 375°. Scrub the potatoes to be sure all the dirt is gone. Then dry them.

2. Poke holes in each potato with a fork.

3. Place the potatoes on a baking sheet and bake them for 1 hour. NOTE: BE SURE TO USE HOT PADS TO REMOVE THE POTATOES FROM THE OVEN. THEY WILL BE VERY HOT!

4. To serve a perfect potato, cut the top with a large X and carefully pull back the skin, being very careful not to burn yourself.

5. Top your potato with anything from the list on the next page and enjoy.

ALSO: Potatoes can be baked one at a time in the microwave oven. Usually a medium potato takes about 8 minutes. So when you are really hungry and just can't wait, bake the potato in the microwave while you are preparing your toppings. (Be sure to poke holes in the potato before you cook it.)

Time to prepare: 3 minutes

Time to bake: 1 hour

Makes 4 servings

Nutrition Information:

One serving	=	1 potato
Calories	=	145
Fat	=	trace
Carbohydrates	=	33 gm.
Protein	=	4 gm.
% Calories from fat	=	1%

Utensils:
Fork,
baking sheet,
hot pads

TATER TOPPERS

When you put different stuff on your potato, you can make it taste different each time. Here are some toppers to try. You can combine them and create your own topper, too. The amounts shown here are for one serving.

1/2 cup low-fat plain yogurt

Calories	=	**62**
Fat	=	**2 gm.**
Carbohydrates	=	**6 gm.**
Protein	=	**4 gm.**
% Calories from fat	=	**31%**

1/2 cup low-fat cottage cheese

Calories	=	**90**
Fat	=	**1 gm.**
Carbohydrates	=	**4 gm.**
Protein	=	**14 gm.**
% Calories from fat	=	**10%**

1/4 cup salsa

Calories	=	**16**
Fat	=	**trace**
Carbohydrates	=	**4 gm.**
Protein	=	**1 gm.**
% Calories from fat	=	**trace**

1/4 cup Butter Buds®, liquid

Calories	=	24
Fat	=	0
Carbohydrates	=	2 gm.
Protein	=	0
% Calories from fat	=	trace

1/2 cup cooked broccoli

Calories	=	35
Fat	=	trace
Carbohydrates	=	6 gm.
Protein	=	4 gm.
% Calories from fat	=	trace

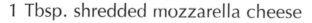

1 Tbsp. shredded mozzarella cheese

Calories	=	45
Fat	=	3 gm.
Carbohydrates	=	trace
Protein	=	5 gm.
% Calories from fat	=	60%

2 Tbsp. shredded cheddar cheese

Calories	=	56
Fat	=	5 gm.
Carbohydrates	=	trace
Protein	=	4 gm.
% Calories from fat	=	73%

Did you notice that some of the toppings have more than 30% of their calories from fat? Try to be very careful with these. Too much fat can throw your pyramid off balance.

POTATO WEDGIES

When you have baked some extra potatoes, try this recipe for a new taste treat.

2	Medium potatoes, already baked
1 Tbsp.	Apple juice or barbecue sauce
1 tsp.	Seasonings like onion powder, garlic powder, or Mrs. Dash®
	Vegetable oil cooking spray

1. Turn on the oven to 400°. Take the baked potatoes you prepared yesterday out of the refrigerator.

2. Slice the potatoes the long way into 4 wedges.

3. Place the potato wedges in a large bowl. Add the apple juice or barbecue sauce. Stir the potatoes with a large spoon until they are all evenly covered with the juice.

4. Use a slotted spoon to put the wedges into another bowl. Sprinkle the seasonings you have chosen over the potato wedges so each wedge is evenly covered.

Set this bowl aside.

Nutrition Information:

One serving	**=**	**4 wedges or 1 potato**
Calories	**=**	**152**
Fat	**=**	**trace**
Carbohydrates	**=**	**35 gm.**
Protein	**=**	**4 gm.**
% Calories from fat	**=**	**1%**

SNACKS

5. Spray a baking sheet with vegetable oil cooking spray.

6. Carefully place the potato wedges on the baking sheet so that no wedge touches another.

7. Bake in the oven for 7 minutes.

8. Carefully take out the baking sheet and turn each wedge over with a pancake turner. BE CAREFUL! THE BAKING SHEET WILL BE VERY HOT. USE A HOT PAD AND SET THE PAN ON A TRIVET OR ANOTHER HOT PAD.

9. Put the baking sheet back into the oven and bake for 7 minutes more. Turn off the oven. Take the baking sheet out of the oven and your Potato Wedgies are ready to eat.

Utensils:
Bowls, large spoon, slotted spoon, baking sheet, pancake turner, hot pads

Time to prepare: 10 minutes

Time to bake: 14 minutes

Makes 2 servings

AFTER-SCHOOL SANDWICHES

Sometimes when you get home, you may want more than just a small snack. Then a sandwich can be a good choice. Here are some of our favorite recipes:

KATIE'S PAINT YOUR PIZZA

This pizza is great after school. It only takes a few minutes to make, and the crust is nice and soft.

1	Pita pocket bread
3 Tbsp.	Pizza or pasta sauce from a jar (like Healthy Choice®)
1/3 cup	Low-fat mozzarella cheese, shredded

1. Put the pita bread on a microwave-safe plate.

2. Use a tablespoon and paint the pocket bread with the sauce.

3. Sprinkle the shredded cheese on top.

4. Place in microwave oven for 1 minute until cheese is melted.

Nutrition Information:

One serving	=	1 pizza
Calories	=	332
Fat	=	9 gm.
Carbohydrates	=	44 gm.
Protein	=	9 gm.
% Calories from fat	=	24

Utensils:
Microwave-safe plate, tablespoon, measuring cup, grater

Time to prepare: 5 minutes

Time to microwave: 1 minute

Makes 1 serving

SORRY CHARLIE SAILBOATS

This tasty tuna is sure to please.

1 6 1/2-oz. can	Water-packed tuna
2 Tbsp.	Celery, finely chopped
2 Tbsp.	Light mayonnaise
2 tsp.	Onion, finely chopped
1 tsp.	Lemon juice
4	Small hamburger buns, unsliced
4	Stalks of celery

1. Drain the tuna and flake it into a medium-sized bowl.

2. Stir in all the remaining ingredients except the hamburger buns and celery.

3. Scoop out the center of each hamburger bun.

4. Stuff each bun with 1/4 cup of the tuna mixture.

5. Put a stalk of celery with leaves in each bun to make it look like a sailboat. Eat and enjoy.

Nutrition Information:

One serving	=	1 sailboat
Calories	=	175
Fat	=	4 gm.
Carbohydrates	=	21 gm.
Protein	=	15 gm.
% Calories from fat	=	21%

Time to prepare: 4 minutes

Makes 4 servings

Utensils:
Can opener, measuring spoons, bowl, fork

OPEN-FACED PIZZAWICH

1 7 1/2-oz. can	Refrigerator biscuits
1/2 cup	Pizza or spaghetti sauce from a jar
2/3 cup	Chopped, cooked ham
2/3 cup	Low-fat mozzarella cheese, shredded

1. Turn on the oven to 400°. On a baking sheet, flatten each biscuit with your fingers until it is twice its original size.

2. Spread 2 teaspoons of sauce over each biscuit.

3. Sprinkle 1 tablespoon of ham over the sauce on each biscuit, and top with 1 tablespoon of cheese.

4. Bake for 8 to 10 minutes.

Nutrition Information:

One serving	=	1 pizza
Calories	=	102
Fat	=	3 gm.
Carbohydrates	=	11 gm.
Protein	=	6 gm.
% Calories from fat	=	26%

Time to prepare:
10 minutes

Time to bake:
8 to 10 minutes

Makes 10 servings

Utensils:
Measuring cups, measuring spoons, baking sheet, hot pads

SNACKS

WHAT TO GRAB WHEN YOU ARE TOO HUNGRY TO WAIT

When you feel so hungry that you just have to have something right now, here are some fast, easy, and good-to-eat snacks.

CINNAMON APPLES FOR FOUR

2	Large red apples
1/4 cup	Sugar
1 tsp.	Cinnamon

1. Combine the cinnamon and the sugar in a small bowl.

2. Pour out 1/4 of the mixture onto each of 4 plates.

3. Cut the apples in half. Then cut each half apple into 4 wedges.

4. Put 4 apple wedges on each plate and let your friends dip the apple into the cinnamon and sugar.

Time to prepare: 2 minutes

Makes 4 servings

Utensils:
Knife, cutting board, measuring cup, measuring spoon, plates

Nutrition Information:

One serving	=	1/2 apple
Calories	=	129
Fat	=	0
Carbohydrates	=	33 gm.
Protein	=	0
% Calories from fat	=	0

SNACKS

105

CRUNCHY CEREAL MIX

Make this in big batches so you have some to grab when you have that too-hungry-to-wait feeling.

1 cup	Wheat Chex®
2 cups	Rice Chex®
1 cup	Corn Chex®
1 cup	Cheerios®
1 cup	Pretzel sticks
1/3 cup	Apple juice
4 tsp.	Worcestershire sauce (ask a grown-up for this)
1/2 tsp.	Garlic powder
1 tsp.	Onion powder

1. Put all the different cereals into a large bowl. Add the pretzel sticks and gently stir it all together. Set it aside.

2. In a measuring cup, mix the apple juice, Worcestershire sauce, garlic powder, and onion powder. Pour it over the cereal mixture.

3. Use a big spoon and stir this all together until all the cereal is covered with some of the sauce.

4. Pour the cereal mixture into a microwave-safe dish. Place the dish in the microwave and cook on high for 2 minutes.

Utensils:
Large bowl, measuring cups, measuring spoons, stirring spoon, microwave-safe dish, bowl, hot pads

5. Very carefully stir the mixture and cook it again on high for 2 more minutes.

6. Stir the mixture again, then turn it on to cook for another 2 minutes.

7. Remove the dish from the microwave carefully. Let it sit for 2 more minutes to cool slightly.

8. Pour the contents into a bowl and serve.

Nutrition Information:

One serving	=	1 cup
Calories	=	103
Fat	=	trace
Carbohydrates	=	37 gm.
Protein	=	2 gm.
% Calories from fat	=	0

Time to prepare: 10 minutes

Time to cook: 6 minutes

Makes 7 servings

SUPER SNACK BARS

Here's another one that's easy to make ahead to have ready when you are.

2 cups	Low-fat granola from the grocery store
1	Egg
2	Egg whites
	Vegetable oil cooking spay

1. Turn on the oven to 350°. Spray an 8-inch square baking pan with vegetable oil cooking spray and set the pan aside.

2. In a bowl, beat the eggs with a whisk or fork. Pour in the granola and stir until the granola is thoroughly coated with the eggs.

3. Pour the mixture into the baking pan and press it down. Put the pan in the oven and bake for 15 minutes.

   BE CAREFUL WHEN YOU TAKE THE PAN OUT. IT WILL BE VERY HOT! USE HOT PADS!

Nutrition Information:

One serving	=	1 bar
Calories	=	95
Fat	=	3 gm.
Carbohydrates	=	17 gm.
Protein	=	3 gm.
% Calories from fat	=	21%

4. Cut the mixture into 8 bars while it is still hot.

5. Use a pancake turner to take the bars out. (They might stick to the pan and they will be quite hot, so be careful.) Set them on a rack to cool.

6. When they are cool, wrap them in aluminum foil or plastic wrap so they are ready to eat later.

Utensils:
Measuring cup, bowl, whisk, 8-inch square baking pan, pancake turner, hot pads, aluminum foil or plastic wrap

Time to prepare:
10 minutes

Time to bake:
15 minutes

Makes
8 servings

YOUR EVENING MEAL

What's the best dinner?

Well, it's time to take a look at your pyramid again. For your total food each day, you want to be sure you have eaten at least 5 servings of the fruits and vegetables group.

In the starch group, the one with the bread, cereal, rice, and pasta, the pyramid shows you should have 6 to 11 servings in a day.

And in the dairy group—that's milk, cheese, and yogurt—you will want to have at least 3 servings in a day. So take a look at your personal chart and see where you are.

Now, how about those fats and sugars? You want to have 6 servings of these each day. Remember, though, that a serving in this food group is very small. It's very easy to eat too many of these foods.

How much food do you need to grow?

If you eat the right amounts of food from the pyramid every day and if you get exercise (that is what you do when you play and do sports), you will have a fine healthy body that will last you for your whole lifetime.

Planning for big events

To help you finish your pyramid plan for each day, we've included some main meal ideas. We'll start off with one that has a lot of complex carbohydrates. (They are the foods at the very bottom of the pyramid, and they include bread, cereal, rice, and pasta.)

When you have a big event coming up, like a soccer game, a baseball play-off, or a race, you'll need to have lots of complex carbohydrates in your body's fuel tank. Pasta is always a great choice for a meal before a sporting event. Here's how to make it yourself.

BASIC SPAGHETTI WITH MEATLESS SAUCE

2 medium	Onions
3 cloves	Garlic
1 Tbsp.	Olive oil
1 6-oz. can	Tomato paste
2 28-oz. cans	Tomatoes
1/2 tsp.	Basil
1/2 tsp.	Marjoram
1/2 tsp.	Thyme
1 pkg.	Spaghetti noodles

Utensils:
Knife, cutting board, measuring spoons, Dutch oven, fork can opener, wooden spoon, colander, saucepan

1. Peel and chop the onions and the garlic. (The garlic should be in very tiny pieces.)

2. Heat the olive oil over medium-low heat in a Dutch oven.

3. When the olive oil is hot, add the onions and garlic. Cook for 6 minutes, stirring occasionally.

4. Stir in the tomato paste and tomatoes. Break up the tomatoes with a fork.

5. Add the basil, marjoram, and thyme.

6. Simmer over medium-low heat for 30 minutes.

7. You can cook the spaghetti noodles while the sauce simmers. The noodles only take about 15 minutes, so wait until the sauce has cooked 15 minutes before you start.

8. When the noodles are cooked, they need to be poured into a colander to drain. BE CAREFUL. GET ADULT HELP TO POUR THE NOODLES. THEY WILL BE VERY HOT WITH LOTS OF STEAM.

9. After the sauce and noodles are both done, serve on plates and enjoy.

You can store the extra sauce in your refrigerator or freeze it. That way you have it ready when you want another high-energy meal.

Time to assemble: 15 minutes

Time to cook: 40 minutes

Makes about 9 servings

Nutrition Information:

One serving	=	3/4 cup
Calories	=	80
Fat	=	2 gm.
Carbohydrates	=	15 gm.
Protein	=	3 gm.
% Calories from fat	=	23%

SIDE-DISH BROILED MEATBALLS

Some people like their spaghetti without meatballs. And some folks like meatballs with their spaghetti. So here's a way you can please everyone.

1 large	Onion
1 lb.	Lean ground beef
1/3 cup	Plain dry bread crumbs
1/3 cup	Grated Parmesan cheese
1/3 cup	Evaporated skim milk
1	Egg
1 1/2 tsp.	Italian seasoning
1 tsp.	Garlic powder
1/2 tsp.	Salt
1/2 tsp.	Pepper
	Vegetable oil cooking spray

1. Peel and chop the onion.

2. Combine all ingredients, except the cooking spray, in a large bowl. Mix it all together.

Utensils:
Cutting board, knife, can opener, large bowl, measuring cups, measuring spoons, 9- by 13-inch baking pan or broiler pan, oven mitts and hot pads, tongs

Time to assemble: 25 minutes

Time to broil: 10 minutes

Makes 5 servings

3. Rinse your hands with water but don't dry them. Use your wet hands to take a small scoop of the meat mixture and roll it around to make a meatball. Do this until you have used all the mixture. You should have 15 meatballs.

4. Carefully place the top oven rack into the slot that is about 7 inches from the top. Then shut the oven and turn on the oven temperature to broil.

5. Spray the baking pan or broiling pan with the vegetable oil cooking spray. Arrange the meatballs in 5 rows across the pan, 3 meatballs to a row.

6. Place the pan on the top oven rack. Shut the oven and set the timer for 5 minutes. When the timer goes off, put on oven mitts, and carefully remove the pan from the broiler. BE CAREFUL. THE BROILER IS THE HOTTEST PART OF THE OVEN AND THE PAN WILL BE EXTREMELY HOT. GET HELP IF YOU NEED IT!

7. Carefully set the hot pan down on two hot pads on the counter. Use tongs to turn each meatball over. When all the meatballs are turned, put the broiler pan back in the oven. BE CAREFUL! USE OVEN MITTS! Set the timer for 5 minutes more.

8. When the timer goes off, carefully remove the pan from the oven. USE OVEN MITTS! Set the broiler or baking pan on hot pads. Close the oven and turn it off. Use the tongs to put the meatballs on a serving dish.

Nutrition Information:

One serving	=	**3 meatballs**
Calories	=	**267**
Fat	=	**13 gm.**
Carbohydrates	=	**10 gm.**
Protein	=	**26 gm.**
% Calories from fat	=	**44%**

ALPHAGHETTI

Here's another high-energy pasta dish. This one has meat in it, but you could make it without.

3/4 cup	Lean ground beef (about 1/2 lb.)
1 15-oz. can	Tomato sauce
1 10 3/4-oz. can	Tomato puree
1 Tbsp.	Beef bouillon granules
1 Tbsp.	Italian seasoning
1 10-oz. pkg.	Alphabet pasta

1. Cook the ground beef in a skillet or frying pan on the stove over medium heat. Separate it with a fork to make it crumbly.

2. Drain the meat through a colander to remove any fat. BE CAREFUL! THE SKILLET WILL BE HOT. USE HOT PADS!

3. Pour the tomato sauce and tomato puree into a 2-quart saucepan. Stir these together. Put the pan on the stove and turn the heat on to medium.

4. Add the beef bouillon, the Italian seasoning, and the hamburger. Stir. Turn the heat to low. Simmer the sauce while you cook the pasta. Give the sauce a stir every few minutes.

Nutrition Information:

One serving	=	1 cup
Calories	=	273
Fat	=	3 gm.
Carbohydrates	=	46 gm.
Protein	=	14 gm.
% Calories from fat	=	12%

MAIN DISHES

5. Pour 3 quarts of water into a large pot. Turn the stove on to high and bring the water to a boil. Pour in the noodles. Bring the water to a boil again and cook for 8 to 10 minutes. Do not cover the pot. Stir the noodles every few minutes.

6. When the noodles are done, drain them by pouring them into a colander. BE CAREFUL. GET ADULT HELP TO POUR THE NOODLES. THEY WILL BE VERY HOT WITH LOTS OF STEAM.

7. Place 1/2 cup of pasta on a plate and cover with 1/2 cup of the spaghetti sauce. Eat and enjoy.

Utensils:
Skillet or frying pan, colander, measuring spoon, can opener, 2-quart saucepan, large pot for pasta, long handled spoon to stir, hot pads

Time to assemble: 15 minutes

Time to cook: 25 minutes

Makes about 6 servings

EASY LASAGNA

Maybe you want your pasta baked instead of cooked on the stove. Here's a recipe for lasagna that's sure to please your whole family.

1 lb.	Lean ground beef
1 large	Onion
2 15-oz. cans	Tomatoes
1 6-oz. can	Tomato paste
1 tsp.	Sugar
1 tsp.	Oregano
1/4 tsp.	Garlic powder
1/2 tsp.	Pepper
8	Lasagna noodles
3 cups	Low-fat cottage cheese, cream style
8 oz.	Low-fat mozzarella cheese, shredded

1. Turn on the oven to 350°.

2. Peel and chop the onion.

3. In a large skillet, brown the ground beef and onion together over medium heat. Separate the meat with a fork to make it crumbly.

4. Carefully pour the meat into a colander to drain it and then return it to the skillet.

5. Add the tomatoes (throw away the liquid and cut up the tomatoes into small chunks), tomato paste, sugar, oregano, garlic powder, and pepper to the skillet with the meat and onions. Mix everything together well.

Time to assemble: 30 minutes

Time to cook: 1 hour and 15 minutes

Makes 8 servings

6. Spoon about half the sauce into a 9- by 13-inch baking dish and spread it with the spoon so the bottom of the pan is covered.

7. Put four of the uncooked noodles in a layer on top of the sauce.

8. Spread all of the cottage cheese over the noodles.

9. Put the last four uncooked noodles over the cottage cheese.

10. Spread the rest of the sauce over the noodles.

11. Sprinkle the mozzarella cheese over the top of the sauce.

12. Cover the pan tightly with foil and bake for 1 hour.

13. Remove the foil from the pan and bake for 15 minutes more. BE CAREFUL! THE PAN IS VERY HOT AND STEAM WILL RISE. YOU SHOULD BE ABLE TO DO THIS WITHOUT TAKING THE PAN OUT OF THE OVEN. BUT IT'S A GOOD IDEA TO ASK FOR HELP!

14. Let the lasagna sit for 15 minutes before you cut it into squares and serve it.

Utensils:
Large skillet, knife, cutting board, colander, spoon, measuring cup, measuring spoons, 9- by 13-inch baking dish, cheese grater, aluminum foil, oven mitts, hot pads

Nutrition Information:

One serving	=	1 cup
Calories	=	435
Fat	=	17 gm.
Carbohydrates	=	29 gm.
Protein	=	41 gm.
% Calories from fat	=	35%

CHICKEN DISHES YOU CAN COOK FOR YOUR FAMILY

When you feel like cooking and you are given permission, here are some chicken dishes to cook for the whole family.

CHICKEN NUGGETS

3	Chicken breasts, skinless and boneless
1 Tbsp.	Flour
1/4 tsp.	Salt
1/4 tsp.	Pepper
2 Tbsp.	Milk (2%)
3/4 cup	Bread crumbs
	Vegetable oil cooking spray

1. Preheat the oven to 425°.

2. Cut the chicken into bite-sized pieces.

3. Combine the flour, salt, and pepper into a small bowl. Put the milk in another small bowl. Pour the bread crumbs into a third bowl. (You should have 3 small bowls on the counter now.)

Nutrition Information:

One serving	=	3 chicken bites
Calories	=	132
Fat	=	2 gm.
Carbohydrates	=	11 gm.
Protein	=	15 gm.
% Calories from fat	=	14%

Time to assemble: 15 minutes

Time to bake: 15 minutes

Makes about 6 servings

4. Dip the chicken into the flour mixture, then into the milk, then into the bread crumbs. Place the chicken bites on a cookie sheet sprayed with vegetable oil cooking spray.

5. Bake in the oven for 15 minutes, until the chicken bites are golden brown and cooked throughout.

Utensils:
Knife, cutting board, 3 small bowls, measuring cup, measuring spoons, cookie sheet, hot pads

REALLY NICE CHICKEN WITH RICE

1 6-oz. can	Orange juice concentrate, thawed
1 pkg.	Dry onion soup mix
3	Chicken breasts, skinless and boneless
1 cup	White or brown rice

1. Turn the oven on to 400°.

2. In a small bowl, gently mix the orange juice with the onion soup mix. Pour half this mixture into a nonstick casserole dish that measures about 8- by 8-inches.

3. Place the chicken breasts in the casserole dish and pour the rest of the sauce over the top.

4. Cover the casserole with a lid or with foil paper. Bake for 1 hour.

5. Cook the rice according to package directions.

Nutrition Information:

One serving	=	1/2 chicken breast over 1/2 cup rice
Calories	=	184
Fat	=	3 gm.
Carbohydrates	=	24 gm.
Protein	=	15 gm.
% Calories from fat	=	14%

6. When the chicken is baked, CAREFULLY TAKE IT OUT OF THE OVEN. (USE HOT PADS OR MITTS.) TURN THE OVEN OFF.

7. Place a scoop of rice in the center of a plate. Cut each chicken breast in half and put a half on top of the rice.

8. Take a small ladle of the sauce from the casserole dish and carefully pour it over the chicken and rice.

Presto! You have a chicken dinner that tastes great and looks very nice on the plate. You could serve this chicken over mashed potatoes or over pasta, too.

Time to assemble: 15 minutes

Time to bake: 1 hour

Makes 6 servings

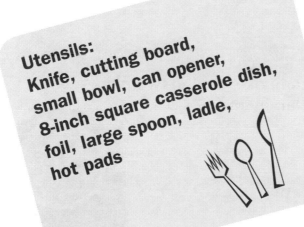

Utensils:
Knife, cutting board, small bowl, can opener, 8-inch square casserole dish, foil, large spoon, ladle, hot pads

FRIENDLY FOWL IN FOIL CHICKEN DINNER BAKE

Did you know that fowl is another word for foods like chicken and turkey? These foods are also called "poultry." This chicken recipe is fun and will really please your family. You make each chicken dinner in aluminum foil and bake the potatoes on the side.

Per person:

1 small to medium	Baking potato
1	Chicken breast, skinless and boneless
1 squirt	Lemon juice from a lemon-shaped juice container
1/2 pinch	Dried parsley, or a pinch of fresh parsley
1/2 pinch	Mrs. Dash seasoning
1	Carrot
1	Celery stalk
1 small	Onion

1. Preheat the oven to 400°.

2. Wash the potatoes and poke them in two places with a fork. Wrap each one in aluminum foil.

Utensils:
Fork, knife, cutting board, aluminum foil, cookie sheet, hot pads

Time to assemble: 15 minutes

Time to bake: 1 hour

3. Wash the chicken breasts. Cut off any yellow pieces of fat.

4. Use a piece of foil about 12 inches long. Place the chicken breast in the center of the foil. Add a squirt of lemon juice. Add the parsley and Mrs. Dash seasoning.

   NOTE: Wash the cutting board thoroughly and use a clean knife to cut the vegetables.

5. Cut the carrot in 1/4 inch slices. Cut the celery in 1/2 inch slices. Cut the onion into thin wedges. Put the vegetables around the chicken breast on the foil.

6. Carefully fold the foil into a tent. Seal all the edges.

7. Place the tent on a cookie sheet and put it in the oven. Put the potatoes on the oven shelf around the cookie sheet.

8. Bake everything for 1 hour. BE CAREFUL! THE COOKIE SHEET AND POTATOES WILL BE VERY HOT WHEN THEY COME OUT OF THE OVEN. USE HOT PADS!

Nutrition Information:

One serving	=	**1 tent meal and 1 potato**
Calories	=	**404**
Fat	=	**3 gm.**
Carbohydrates	=	**61 gm.**
Protein	=	**33 gm.**
% Calories from fat	=	**6%**

FISH IS FUN FOOD TO COOK AND TO EAT

Fish is very good for your body. It gives you lots of fuel without a lot of the fat that is not so good for your body. Here are a couple of our favorite fish recipes that you can cook for dinner.

FISH IN A FLASH

Here's a way to cook fish in the microwave that is as fast as heating up those frozen fish sticks, and it is better for your body.

4 4-oz. each	Fillets of flounder, orange roughy, cod, or any mild fish (thawed if you bought it frozen)
1/4 tsp.	Salt
8 large	Whole-wheat crackers
2 Tbsp.	Margarine
1 1/2 tsp.	Fresh lemon juice
1 Tbsp.	Freshly chopped parsley, or 1/2 Tbsp. dried

1. Rinse the fish fillets and pat them dry with a paper towel.

2. Sprinkle the fish lightly with salt on both sides.

Utensils:
Paper towels, measuring spoons, microwave-safe baking dish, rolling pin and resealable plastic bag, plastic wrap, microwave-safe measuring cup, medium bowl, spoon, hot pads, fork

3. Place the fillets in one layer in a microwave-safe baking dish.

4. Put the crackers in a strong, sealed, plastic bag and roll over them with a rolling pin until they are smashed into small fine crumbs.

5. Melt the margarine in a microwave-safe measuring cup and pour it into a medium-sized bowl.

6. Add the cracker crumbs, lemon juice and parsley to the bowl. Stir to mix everything together.

7. Use a spoon to sprinkle the crumb mixture over the top of the fish fillets. Cover the dish with its lid or with plastic wrap.

8. Microwave on high for 6 to 7 minutes. The fish is done when it flakes after you poke it in the center with a fork. BE CAREFUL! THIS WILL BE HOT!

Be sure to use hot pads or oven mitts when you remove the dish from the microwave. It will be very hot. Also, be careful when you lift the lid or remove the plastic wrap. There will be steam. Always open lids away from your face.

Time to assemble: 15 minutes

Time to microwave: 6 to 7 minutes

Makes 4 servings

Nutrition Information:

One serving	=	1 fish fillet
Calories	=	243
Fat	=	9 gm.
Carbohydrates	=	6 gm.
Protein	=	31 gm.
% Calories from fat	=	33%

CREAMY TUNA ON TOAST

Tuna is always a good choice. Buy the white kind, packed in water.

1 6 1/8-oz. can	Tuna, packed in water
1 Tbsp.	Margarine
1 Tbsp.	Flour
1 cup	Milk (2%)
1/4 tsp.	Mustard (from a jar)
4 slices	Whole-wheat bread

1. Open tuna. Pour it into a colander in the sink to drain.

2. Put margarine in a medium saucepan and melt over low heat.

3. Add flour and stir with a fork to blend. This will be thick and look like a paste.

4. Pour in about 1/4 cup of milk. Use a wire whisk to stir the paste into it. Add the rest of the milk and stir with the whisk.

5. Stir in the mustard.

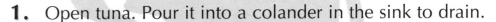

Nutrition Information:

One serving	=	1 slice toast with 1/4 of the tuna
Calories	=	122
Fat	=	4 gm.
Carbohydrates	=	12 gm.
Protein	=	10 gm.
% Calories from fat	=	29%

6. Add the tuna and cook over low heat for 10 minutes. Stir this mixture every few minutes to keep it from burning on the bottom of the pan. It if starts bubbling a lot, turn the heat down to low and finish cooking.

7. While the tuna is cooking, toast the bread. (Don't butter the bread.)

8. To serve, put one piece of toast on each plate and spoon the tuna over it.

Time to assemble: 15 minutes

Time to cook: 10 minutes

Makes 4 servings

Utensils:
Can opener, fork, colander, wire whisk, measuring spoons, measuring cup, toaster, saucepan

CHINESE STIR-FRY WITH SHRIMP

Stir-frying is a fun way to cook, but you may want to have a grown-up help you. The wok, the large frying pan in which you stir fry, gets very hot.

1 1/2 cups	Frozen broccoli florets, or cut fresh broccoli
1 1/2 cups	Frozen whole baby carrots
1 small	Green onion
2 Tbsp.	Honey
1 Tbsp.	Fresh lemon juice
1/8 tsp.	Ground allspice
1/8 to 1/4 tsp.	Ground ginger
Pinch	Black pepper
2 tsp.	Margarine
1 tsp.	Sesame oil
1/2 lb. medium	Shrimp, cleaned and thawed

1. Place the frozen broccoli and carrots in the colander. Run hot water over them until they are defrosted. This should take about 1 minute. Let all the water drain out of the colander, then pour the vegetables onto paper towels so they get very dry. Pat them with the paper towels to get the tops dry, too.

2. Cut the carrots into thin diagonal slices. Set them aside.

Utensils:
Measuring cups, colander, paper towels, cutting board, knife, 2 small bowls, measuring spoons, wok or deep skillet, oven mitt or hot pad, wooden stirring spoon

3. Wash and slice the green part of the onion. Throw the white part away. Measure 1 teaspoon of the onion and put it in a small bowl.

4. Place the honey, lemon juice, allspice, ginger, and pepper in another small bowl. Set it aside.

5. Put the margarine and the sesame oil into the wok or a deep skillet. Turn the heat to medium-high. Heat the margarine and oil until it is very hot. THIS IS A GOOD PLACE TO ASK FOR HELP FROM A GROWN-UP. WOKS CAN GET VERY HOT!

6. Carefully put the cleaned, thawed shrimp into the wok. Stir it with a long-handled spatula made especially for the wok or with a wooden spatula. Hold the handle of the wok with a hot pad in one hand, and stir with a wooden spatula with your other hand. You need to keep stirring and stirring for about 3 minutes until all the shrimp is cooked. It will change from looking kind of glassy to looking kind of papery.

7. Carefully add the broccoli, carrots, and green onion to the wok. Cook another 2 minutes, stirring all the time.

8. Add the honey and lemon mixture. Cook 2 to 3 minutes longer, stirring all the time.

9. Serve. The vegetables should be crispy and crunchy. The shrimp should be pinkish white and slightly chewy.

Time to assemble: 25 minutes

Time to cook: 7 to 8 minutes

Makes 4 servings

Nutrition Information:

One serving	=	1/4 recipe
Calories	=	113
Fat	=	6 gm.
Carbohydrates	=	13 gm.
Protein	=	14 gm.
% Calories from fat	=	31%

SIDE-DISH POTATOES

Potatoes always make a good side dish. So do rice and pasta. The directions for cooking rice and pasta can be found on the package. The recipe for baked potatoes is on page 97. You can also serve potatoes in a salad by using the recipe below.

POTATO SALAD

Try this recipe with your Chicken Nuggets.

14 medium	Red-skinned potatoes
8 cups	Water
1/4 tsp.	Salt
1	Egg
4 stalks	Celery
1/2 cup	Onion
4 Tbsp.	Light mayonnaise
1 tsp.	Dijon mustard
1 Tbsp.	Milk (2%)
1/4 tsp.	Pepper

1. Scrub the potatoes but don't peel them. Cut each potato into 1/2-inch chunks.

2. Put 8 cups of water in a Dutch oven over high heat.

3. Add potatoes and salt. Bring to a low boil and boil for about 15 minutes. Potatoes are done when you can stick a fork into one without pushing very hard. If you are in doubt, take a piece of potato out, cool it, and taste it. It should be just a little chewy.

Utensils:
Knife, cutting board, measuring cup, measuring spoons, large bowl, small saucepan, small bowl, wooden spoon, fork, Dutch oven, colander

4. While the potatoes are cooking, fill a small saucepan with cool water and put in the egg. Put this on the stove over medium heat until the water boils. When the water starts to boil, set the timer for 4 minutes.

5. When the timer goes off, turn off the stove. Let the egg sit in the water for 2 more minutes. Then carefully pour the water and the egg into a colander over the sink. Let the egg cool for at least 10 minutes.

6. When the potatoes are cooked, pour them into the colander over the sink. BE CAREFUL! THIS PART IS HEAVY AND HOT. YOU MAY WANT TO GET HELP FROM A GROWN-UP OR YOU CAN LET THE POTATOES COOL BEFORE YOU DRAIN THEM.

7. Put the drained potatoes into a large bowl.

8. Chop the celery, onion, and egg and add them to the potatoes.

9. In a small bowl, stir the mayonnaise, Dijon mustard, milk and pepper together.

10. Pour this mixture over the potatoes and eggs and stir it around gently until all the potatoes are coated.

11. Chill for 1/2 hour and serve.

Nutrition Information:

One serving = 1/2 cup
Calories = 132
Fat = 1 gm.
Carbohydrates = 29 gm.
Protein = 3 gm.
% Calories from fat = 7%

Time to assemble: 15 minutes

Time to cook: 15 minutes

Time to chill: 30 minutes

Makes 14 servings

MAIN DISHES

133

BAKED TOMATOES

Did you know that tomatoes are really a fruit and not a vegetable? It doesn't really matter, but it is interesting. And here is an interesting way to bake tomatoes to serve on the side with any main meal menu.

4 medium	
to large	Tomatoes
2 tsp.	Grated Parmesan cheese
4 tsp.	Bread crumbs
	Vegetable oil cooking spray
Pinch	Salt

1. Turn on the oven to 450°.

2. Wash the tomatoes.

3. Cut the top off each tomato. Put the tomatoes on a cookie sheet.

4. Sprinkle 1/2 teaspoon of Parmesan cheese onto each tomato.

5. Sprinkle 1 teaspoon of bread crumbs onto each tomato.

Nutrition Information:

One serving	=	1 tomato
Calories	=	26
Fat	=	trace
Carbohydrates	=	6 gm.
Protein	=	1 gm.
% Calories from fat	=	trace

6. Spray the tops of the tomatoes with vegetable oil cooking spray, two sprays for each tomato.

7. Bake the tomatoes for 20 minutes. BE CAREFUL! THE COOKIE SHEET WILL BE VERY HOT WHEN IT COMES OUT OF THE OVEN. USE OVEN MITTS OR HOT PADS, OR GET A GROWN-UP TO HELP YOU!

8. Sprinkle each tomato with a little pinch of salt once they are out of the oven. Use a spatula to move them onto a plate. They are ready to serve.

Time to assemble: 10 minutes

Time to cook: 20 minutes

Makes 4 servings

Utensils:
Knife, cutting board, measuring spoons, hot pads, cookie sheet, spatula

CHEESY GREEN BEANS

1 16-oz. can	Green beans
1/2 cup	Soft cheese spread

1. Drain the beans and pour them into a small microwave-safe bowl.
2. Add the soft cheese, and microwave on high power for 2 minutes.
3. Stir to mix.
4. Serve.

Time to assemble: 5 minutes

Time to cook: 2 minutes

Makes 4 servings

Nutrition Information:

One serving	=	1/2 cup
Calories	=	101
Fat	=	6 gm.
Carbohydrates	=	7 gm.
Protein	=	5 gm.
% Calories from fat	=	49%

Utensils:
Can opener,
strainer or colander,
microwave-safe bowl

SALADS AND DRESSINGS

In addition to the previous main meal menus, you may want to add some more vegetables to fill out your pyramid. Here are some recipes that will please all the bodies in your house.

TOSSED SALADS

That Tossed Super Salad recipe on page 66 is terrific on the side at your main meal. Here are some recipes for tasty salad dressings that will make your salad different each time.

BUTTERMILK DRESSING

1/2 cup	Low-fat buttermilk
1 Tbsp.	White wine vinegar with 1/2 tsp. sugar added
2 tsp.	Dijon mustard
1/4 tsp.	Salt
1/4 tsp.	Pepper
3	Green onions, thinly sliced
1	Clove garlic, minced or pressed

Time to assemble: 5 minutes

Time to chill: 10 minutes

Makes 12 servings

1. Mix all ingredients together.

2. Refrigerate for about 10 minutes before serving.

Nutrition Information:

One serving	=	1 Tbsp.
Calories	=	9
Fat	=	trace
Carbohydrates	=	1 gm.
Protein	=	trace
% Calories from fat	=	4%

Utensils:
Knife, cutting board, garlic press, measuring cup, measuring spoons, small bowl

BASIC FRENCH DRESSING

1 tsp.	Salt
1/2 tsp.	Paprika
1/2 tsp.	Pepper
1/2 tsp.	Dry mustard
1/4 tsp.	Sugar
1/4 tsp.	Garlic powder
1/2 cup	Olive oil
1/4 cup	Red wine vinegar (white wine vinegar or plain vinegar will also work)

1. Measure all the dry ingredients into a large measuring cup or small bowl. Use a spoon to grind them against the side of the cup or bowl until they are well mixed and powdery.

2. And add the oil and vinegar.

Time to
assemble:
10 minutes

Time to chill:
10 minutes

Makes
24 servings

Utensils:
Measuring cup, measuring spoons, small bowl, beater, bottle

MAIN DISHES

3. Use a hand-held beater and mix well.

4. Put the dressing in a bottle, cover it, and refrigerate it for about 10 minutes. Shake it up and it is ready to use.

Nutrition Information:

One serving	=	1/2 Tbsp.
Calories	=	41
Fat	=	4 gm.
Carbohydrates	=	0
Protein	=	0
% Calories from fat	=	99%

STRAWBERRY DRESSING

1 1/2 cups	Strawberries, washed and hulled
1/4 cup	Lemon juice
1 Tbsp.	Sugar
1 Tbsp.	Finely chopped shallot (a teeny onion)
1/2 tsp.	Dry tarragon
1/2 tsp.	Cornstarch
2 Tbsp.	Orange Juice

1. Put the strawberries in the blender, and turn the blender on to puree.

2. Pour the strawberries through a fine mesh strainer into a 2-cup measuring cup.

3. Add the lemon juice and enough water to make 1 cup.

4. Pour this cup of liquid into a small saucepan and add the sugar, shallot, and tarragon.

5. In a small bowl, mix the cornstarch and orange juice together until they are smooth.

Utensils:
Blender, measuring cups, fine strainer, small saucepan, measuring spoons, small bowl

6. Turn on the stove to medium-high heat and carefully stir the cornstarch and orange juice mixture into the strawberry mixture.

7. Bring this to a boil over high heat. Stir it all the time.

8. Carefully remove the pan from the heat. Turn off the stove, and put the pan into a bowl of ice water so that it chills quickly.

9. After the dressing has cooled off, taste it. Does it need more lemon juice? Add a little more if you want.

10. The dressing is ready to serve.

Nutrition Information:

One serving	=	1/2 Tbsp.
Calories	=	10
Fat	=	trace
Carbohydrates	=	2 gm.
Protein	=	trace
% Calories from fat	=	5%

Time to assemble: 15 minutes

Time to cook: 3 minutes

Time to chill: 10 minutes

Makes 24 servings

THREE FRUIT SALAD

Sometimes you feel like eating a fresh fruit salad with your main meal instead of a lettuce salad. Here's a really refreshing one that could be a lunch all by itself.

1 can	Unsweetened pineapple chunks
1 cup	Strawberries
1 small	Golden Delicious apple
1/3 cup	Plain low-fat yogurt
8	Nice lettuce leaves
8	Whole strawberries
1 cup	Low-fat, small-curd cottage cheese

1. Open the pineapple can and pour it into a colander over the sink to drain.

2. Wash the strawberries, and cut them into halves.

3. Wash the apple, then cut it in half and take out the core. Cut the apple into 1/2-inch pieces.

4. Pour the pineapple chunks, the apple pieces, and the strawberry halves into a medium-sized bowl. Cover them with the yogurt, and stir this mixture gently with a large spoon.

5. Cover the bowl with plastic wrap and place it in the refrigerator for 10 minutes.

Utensils:
Can opener, colander, knife, cutting board, measuring cup, large spoon, medium bowl, plastic wrap, tablespoon, salad plates

6. Wash and dry the 8 lettuce leaves. Wash the 8 whole strawberries.

7. Place a lettuce leaf on each of 8 salad plates. Then put a whole strawberry on the lettuce leaf over to the side of the plate.

8. Spoon 1/8th of the fruit salad onto the center of the lettuce leaf on each plate.

9. Add 2 tablespoons of cottage cheese to the top of each fruit salad and serve.

Time to assemble: 15 minutes

Time to chill: 10 minutes

Makes 8 servings

Nutrition Information:

One serving	=	about 1 cup
Calories	=	92
Fat	=	2 gm.
Carbohydrates	=	16 gm.
Protein	=	4 gm.
% Calories from fat	=	17%

YOKOTA SALAD

Here's a salad for you with a really funny name. But don't let the name fool you. You'll love to make this.

1/3 medium head	Cabbage
4 leaves	Romaine lettuce
1 medium	Carrot, grated
2 leaves	Fresh basil
8 large leaves	Parsley
5 leaves	Chives
2 Tbsp.	Rice vinegar
1 Tbsp.	Sesame oil, the light-colored kind
3/4 tsp.	Soy sauce

1. Wash the cabbage. Cut out a wedge that equals about 1/3 of the cabbage. This cutting can be tricky, so ask a grown-up for help.

2. Cut the cabbage into slices about 1/16th-inch thick (this is thin, like in coleslaw). Put the sliced cabbage into a salad bowl.

Time to assemble: 15 minutes

Makes 9 servings

Utensils:
Knife, cutting board, grater, measuring cup, scissors, measuring spoons, salad bowl

3. Wash the romaine lettuce and tear it into bite-sized pieces. Add it to the salad bowl with the cabbage.

4. Scrub the carrot and grate it into the salad bowl.

5. Wash the basil, parsley, and chives and use a scissors to cut them up into very small pieces. Add them to the bowl.

6. Combine the rice vinegar, sesame oil, and soy sauce in a measuring cup. Pour this mixture over the salad and toss the salad until it is well coated with the sauce.

Nutrition Information:

One serving	=	3/4 cup
Calories	=	24
Fat	=	2 gm.
Carbohydrates	=	2 gm.
Protein	=	1 gm.
% Calories from fat	=	75% (but of just 24 calories!)

AND FOR DESSERT

Sometimes it's nice to end the meal with a little something sweet to eat. Here are some of our favorite recipes for dessert.

APPLE CRISP

4 medium	Apples (Granny Smiths are great!)
Juice from	1/2 a lemon
1/3 cup	Water
1 cup	Rolled oats
1/2 cup	Flour (you can use white or whole wheat)
1 tsp.	Cinnamon
1/4 tsp.	Salt
1/2 cup	Brown sugar, packed
2 Tbsp.	Honey
1/4 cup	Corn oil

1. Preheat the oven to 350°.

2. Wash, then slice the apples into thin slices. (Be sure to take out the core.)

3. Put the apple slices into a 9-inch square baking pan. Put the lemon juice and water over the apples, and stir to be sure they are all coated with the liquid.

Utensils:
Knife, cutting board, measuring cup, measuring spoons, medium bowl, wooden spoon, 9-inch square baking pan, hot pads

MAIN DISHES

4. In a medium-sized bowl, stir the oats and flour together. Add the cinnamon and salt. Stir again.

5. Measure the brown sugar and add it to the oats. Use your fingers to break up any lumps in the brown sugar.

6. Add the honey and corn oil and stir. Make sure the oil coats all the oats and flour.

7. Sprinkle the oat mixture over the apples.

8. Put the pan in the oven and bake it for 45 minutes. BE CAREFUL WHEN YOU TAKE THE PAN OUT! USE HOT PADS! IT WILL BE VERY HOT!

Time to assemble:
15 minutes

Time to bake:
45 minutes

Makes 6 servings

Nutrition Information:

One serving	=	1/6 of recipe
Calories	=	293
Fat	=	10 gm.
Carbohydrates	=	49 gm.
Protein	=	3 gm.
% Calories from fat	=	31%

WOBBLY FRUIT

This recipe calls for gelatin, but it doesn't mean JELL-O®. You can find envelopes of unflavored gelatin in the baking section of the grocery store.

1 Tbsp.	Gelatin powder, unflavored
2 Tbsp.	Cold water
1/2 cup	Boiling water
1 1/2 cups	Sugar-free ginger ale
2 Tbsp.	Lemon juice
1/4 cup	Sugar
1 cup	Strawberries
1/2 cup	Seedless grapes
1 cup	Bananas

1. Put the gelatin and 2 tablespoons of cold water into a bowl. Stir to dissolve the gelatin. Add boiling water. Stir again until the gelatin is completely dissolved.

2. Add the ginger ale, lemon juice, and sugar. Put the bowl into the refrigerator for 2 hours.

Time to assemble:
15 minutes

Time to chill:
8 hours

Makes
6 servings

Utensils:
Measuring cup, measuring spoons, medium bowl, gelatin mold or glass bowl, knife, cutting board

3. Wash the strawberries, then cut them into small bites. Wash the grapes and cut them in half. The strawberries and grapes can be cut up early.

4. Peel the bananas and slice them into 1/8 inch rounds. The banana has to be cut just before you are ready to use it or it will turn brown.

5. Stir the fruit into the gelatin. Pour the mixture into a gelatin mold or a medium-sized glass dish. Refrigerate it until the mixture is firm.

Nutrition Information:

One serving	=	1/2 cup
Calories	=	72
Fat	=	trace
Carbohydrates	=	17 gm.
Protein	=	1 gm.
% Calories from fat	=	3%

Aloha Flip

It's not a pudding, and not a cake, but it's good and it's easy!

1 20-oz. can	Crushed pineapple
1 cup	Sugar
1 cup	Milk (2%)
1 cup	Flour
2 tsp.	Baking powder
1 Tbsp.	Margarine
1 tsp.	Vanilla extract
	Vegetable oil cooking spray

1. Preheat oven to 375°.

2. Spray an 8-inch or 9-inch square cake pan with vegetable oil cooking spray.

3. Drain the pineapple but save the juice.

4. Spread pineapple across the bottom of the greased cake pan.

5. Mix the sugar, milk, flour, and baking powder together.

6. Pour the batter over the pineapple.

Utensils:
Measuring cup, measuring spoons, small saucepan, medium bowl, can opener, colander, 8-inch or 9-inch cake pan, hot pads

7. Put the margarine, vanilla, and left-over pineapple juice in a saucepan over medium heat. Heat until the margarine melts. Stir to blend.

8. Pour the juice over the batter.

9. Bake for 45 minutes.

   BE CAREFUL WHEN YOU TAKE THIS OUT OF THE OVEN. IT WILL BE VERY HOT! USE OVEN MITTS OR HOT PADS!

10. Serve this cake hot. It's especially good with a little milk poured over it.

Time to assemble:
15 minutes

Time to bake:
45 minutes

Makes
6 servings

Nutrition Information:

One serving	=	1/6 part
Calories	=	301
Fat	=	3 gm.
Carbohydrates	=	66 gm.
Protein	=	4 gm.
% Calories from fat	=	9%

EZ ORANGE SHERBET

Here's an easy dessert to try.

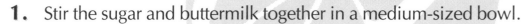

1 1/2 cups	Sugar
2 cups	Buttermilk
1 cup	Orange juice

1. Stir the sugar and buttermilk together in a medium-sized bowl.

2. Add the orange juice and stir again.

3. Pour it into a 9- by 13-inch glass dish. Put the dish in the freezer.

4. In about 3 hours, take the sherbet out of the freezer. Scoop it out of the pan and use an electric mixer to beat it. Then put it back in the glass dish and return it to the freezer. This makes it creamier. If you forget to do this, it will still taste good, but it will have more ice crystals in it.

Utensils:
Measuring cup, medium bowl, 9- by 13-inch glass dish, wooden spoon, electric mixer

Time to assemble: 10 minutes

Time to freeze: 5 to 6 hours

Makes 8 servings

Nutrition Information:

One serving	=	1/2 cup
Calories	=	197
Fat	=	1 gm.
Carbohydrates	=	47 gm.
Protein	=	3 gm.
% Calories from fat	=	4%

SPECIAL STUFF

SPECIAL OCCASIONS AND BAKING DAYS

Sometimes you want to spend time in the kitchen and just enjoy the adventure of it. Special occasions, like Mother's Day or Father's Day, are good times to try your best to surprise your family. Here are some recipes for special days.

BAKED GOODS

Baking usually takes a little more time in the kitchen and should be done when a grown-up can help you. You can bake up a bunch of stuff on a Saturday and have something special for breakfast, lunch, or dinner during the rest of the week.

GINGERBREAD MUFFIN MIX

These muffins can be used for breakfast or for dessert! They taste best, just like gingerbread, right out of the oven. Make as many muffins as you want and store the rest of the batter in the refrigerator for up to a week.

1/2 cup	Margarine
1 cup	Sugar
4	Eggs
1 tsp.	Vanilla extract
1 cup	Molasses
1 tsp.	Baking soda dissolved in 1 Tbsp. hot water
3 1/2 cups	Flour
1 tsp.	Nutmeg
1 Tbsp.	Ginger
1 1/2 cups	Buttermilk

1. Preheat the oven to 350°.

2. Using an electric mixer, cream the margarine and sugar together.

3. Break the eggs into a small bowl. Beat the eggs until they are well blended but not frothy.

Nutrition Information:

One serving	=	1 muffin
Calories	=	149
Fat	=	6 gm.
Carbohydrates	=	22 gm.
Protein	=	2 gm.
% Calories from fat	=	36%

SPECIAL OCCASIONS

4. Add eggs to margarine and sugar and mix.

5. Add vanilla, molasses, and baking soda to the mixture.

6. Measure flour into another bowl. Add nutmeg and ginger. Stir together, being sure to break up any lumps in the ginger.

7. Pour 1/2 of the flour mixture and 1/2 of the buttermilk into another bowl. Use a wooden spoon, not the mixer, to stir until you just have small lumps left. Add the other half of the buttermilk and the flour, and stir again.

8. Combine the two mixtures together.

9. Put paper liners in the muffin tins. Fill each muffin cup 1/2 full with batter.

10. Bake for 20 minutes.

NOTE: BE SURE TO USE HOT PADS WHEN YOU TAKE ANYTHING OUT OF THE OVEN. THE MUFFIN TINS WILL BE VERY HOT.

Time to assemble: 25 minutes

Time to bake: 20 minutes

Makes 36 servings

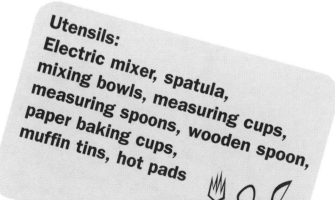

Utensils:
Electric mixer, spatula, mixing bowls, measuring cups, measuring spoons, wooden spoon, paper baking cups, muffin tins, hot pads

BEETLE MUFFINS

Here's a tasty snack that's not just for breakfast. Take this on the school bus and tease your friends by telling them you put beetles and bugs in the muffins where the raisins are.

2	Egg whites
1 1/4 cups	Milk (2%)
1/2 cup	Applesauce
1 cup	Whole wheat flour
2 cups	100% bran cereal
1/3 cup	Brown sugar, packed
2 tsp.	Baking powder
1/2 cup	Baking soda
1/2 tsp.	Cinnamon
1/2 tsp.	Nutmeg
72	Raisins (your pretend beetles)

1. Preheat the oven to 400°.

2. In a large bowl, use an egg separator to separate the yolks from the egg whites. Put the yolks in a small covered bowl and store in the refrigerator.

3. Mix the egg whites, milk, and applesauce together.

Utensils:
Egg separator, large bowl, small bowl, measuring cups, measuring spoons, wooden mixing spoon, paper baking cups, muffin tins, hot pads

4. Add the flour, bran cereal, brown sugar, baking powder, baking soda, and spices. Stir with a wooden spoon until you just have small lumps left.

5. Place paper liners in muffin tins and fill to 2/3 full with batter.

6. Push 3 raisins into the center of each muffin. Put 3 more around the top of each muffin.

7. Bake until the muffins are slightly brown. This takes about 20 minutes.

   NOTE: BE SURE TO USE HOT PADS WHEN YOU TAKE ANYTHING OUT OF THE OVEN. THE MUFFIN TINS WILL BE VERY HOT.

Nutrition Information:

One serving	=	1 muffin
Calories	=	128
Fat	=	1 gm.
Carbohydrates	=	28 gm.
Protein	=	4 gm.
% Calories from fat	=	7%

Time to assemble: 25 minutes

Time to bake: about 20 minutes

Makes 12 servings

BANANARAMA MUFFINS

These are a real treat we are sure you'll simply love to eat.

1 cup	Whole-wheat flour
2 1/2 tsp.	Baking powder
3/4 cup	Quick rolled oats
1/4 tsp.	Salt
1/4 tsp.	Baking soda
1	Egg white
3 Tbsp.	Honey
1/2 cup	Milk (2%)
1 Tbsp.	Vegetable oil
2 ripe	Bananas, mashed

1. Heat the oven to 400°.

2. Combine the flour, baking powder, rolled oats, salt, and baking soda in a large bowl. Set the bowl aside.

3. Use an egg separator to separate the yolk from the white of the egg. Add the egg white to the flour mixture, but DO NOT mix.

Time to assemble: 25 minutes

Time to bake: 18 to 20 minutes

Makes 12 servings

4. Add honey, milk, oil, and bananas to the flour mixture. Stir everything together with a fork until the dry parts are wet.

5. Put paper liners in muffin tins. Fill liners about two-thirds full with batter.

6. Bake until the muffins are slightly brown, about 18 to 20 minutes.

NOTE: BE SURE YOU USE HOT PADS WHEN YOU TAKE SOMETHING OUT OF A HOT OVEN. YOU DON'T WANT TO BURN YOURSELF.

Utensils:
Egg separator, large bowl, measuring cups, measuring spoons, fork, paper baking cups, muffin tins, hot pads

Nutrition Information:

One serving	=	1 muffin
Calories	=	101
Fat	=	2 gm.
Carbohydrates	=	18 gm.
Protein	=	3 gm.
% Calories from fat	=	16%

BAKE-IT-YOURSELF BANANA BREAD

When you have some time and there's a grown-up around to give you a hand, try baking this special bread. Baking bread can be fun, and this bread is neat to eat as a special treat!

1 cup	Sugar
1/2 cup	Sour cream, nonfat
2	Eggs
3	Bananas
2 cups	White flour
1/2 tsp.	Baking soda
1/2 tsp.	Baking powder
	Vegetable oil cooking spray
1/2 cup	Pecans or walnuts (buy them chopped or, if you aren't nutty for nuts, leave them out)

1. Preheat the oven to 350°.

2. Blend the sugar and sour cream in a large mixing bowl with an electric mixer.

3. Add the eggs. Peel and slice the bananas. Use the mixer to mash and mix in the bananas.

Utensils:
Large mixing bowl, knife, cutting board, electric mixer, small bowl, measuring spoons, measuring cups, wooden spoon, 9- by 5-inch loaf pan, toothpick, hot pads

4. In a small bowl, mix the flour, baking soda, and baking powder.

5. Add half the flour mixture to the banana mixture. Use a low speed on the mixer and mix just enough to get the flour wet.

6. Add the rest of the flour the same way. Stop mixing as soon as all the flour is mixed in.

7. If you want to add nuts, now is the time. Stir them in with a wooden spoon.

8. Spray a 9- by 5-inch loaf pan with vegetable oil cooking spray.

9. Pour the bread batter into the loaf pan, put it into the oven, and bake it for one hour or until a toothpick inserted in the center comes out clean.

10. Cool your bread for half an hour before slicing and serving.

Time to assemble: 20 minutes

Time to bake: 1 hour

Makes 12 servings

Nutrition Information:

One serving = 1/12 loaf

	With nuts	Without nuts
Calories	218	183
Fat	5 gm.	1 gm.
Carbohydrates	41 gm.	40 gm.
Protein	5 gm.	4 gm.
% Calories from fat	21%	5%

Fine And Fancy Breakfast or Brunch Feasts

Here are some ideas for times when you want to cook breakfast or brunch for the grown-ups in your house.

Mighty Fine French Toast

2	Egg whites
2 Tbsp.	Milk (2%)
1/4 tsp.	Vanilla extract
1/8 tsp.	Cinnamon
1 slice	Whole-wheat bread
	Vegetable oil cooking spray

Nutrition Information:

One serving	=	**1 slice**
Calories	=	**96**
Fat	=	**trace**
Carbohydrates	=	**13 gm.**
Protein	=	**10 gm.**
% Calories from fat	=	**trace**

1. Use an egg separator to separate the yolks from the egg whites. Put the egg yolks in a small dish, cover, and place in refrigerator.

2. In an 8-inch square baking pan, combine egg whites, milk, vanilla extract, and cinnamon. Beat lightly with a wire whisk.

3. Spray a large griddle or frying pan with vegetable oil cooking spray. Put the frying pan on the stove and turn the stove on to medium. (You can also use an electric griddle set at 400°.)

4. Dip the slice of bread into the egg mixture. Be sure to soak both sides of the bread. Then place it on the griddle or in the frying pan. Cook it until it is golden brown on one side, then flip it over with a pancake turner and cook the other side until it is golden brown.

5. Be sure to turn off the stove.

Time to assemble:
10 minutes

Time to fry:
about 6 minutes

Makes
1 serving

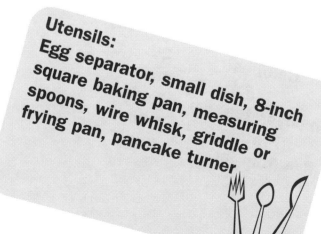

Utensils:
Egg separator, small dish, 8-inch square baking pan, measuring spoons, wire whisk, griddle or frying pan, pancake turner

Sweet And Chunky Toast Topper

Here's a recipe for a delicious fruit topping for your French toast or your pancakes. It is made in stages, so it's fun, and the sauce you get at the end is delicious.

2 cups	Fresh fruit (try strawberries, raspberries, peaches, or cherries)
2 Tbsp.	Cornstarch
1/2 cup	Water

1. Chop the fruit into large pieces.

2. Mix the cornstarch with the water and use a whisk to stir it together. Put it in a small saucepan and heat it on the stove until it is boiling.

3. Add 1 cup of the chopped fruit to the saucepan and stir it until it boils again. (Note: Remember boiling is another word for bubbling.)

Nutrition Information:

One serving	=	1/4 cup
Calories	=	20
Fat	=	trace
Carbohydrates	=	5 gm.
Protein	=	trace
% Calories from fat	=	6%

4. As soon as it boils, take it off the stove and put it on a trivet or a hot pad. Add the fruit that is left and stir.

You can serve this hot or put the mixture into the refrigerator and serve it cold later. Its fun to make and sweet to eat.

Time to
assemble:
10 minutes

Time to cook:
about 10
minutes

Makes
10 servings

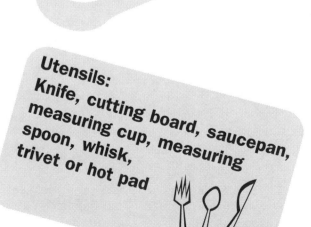

Utensils:
Knife, cutting board, saucepan,
measuring cup, measuring
spoon, whisk,
trivet or hot pad

FRENCH TOAST FOR FRIENDS

For those special nights when you have friends sleep over, try fixing this the night before so breakfast is ready when you wake up.

6	3/4-inch slices French bread
1	Egg
4	Egg whites
2 cups	Milk (2%)
3/4 tsp.	Cinnamon
	Vegetable oil cooking spray

1. Spray a 9- by 13-inch baking pan with vegetable oil cooking spray. Arrange the bread slices in the baking pan and set the pan aside.

2. Use an egg separator to separate yolks from egg whites. In a small bowl, use a whisk to stir the whole egg, egg whites, milk, and cinnamon together.

3. Pour the egg mixture over the slices of bread in the baking pan.

Nutrition Information:

One serving	=	1 slice
Calories	=	116
Fat	=	2 gm.
Carbohydrates	=	17 gm.
Protein	=	8 gm.
% Calories from fat	=	14%

4. Cover the baking pan with plastic wrap. Put it in the refrigerator overnight.

5. In the morning, remove the plastic wrap from the baking pan. Put the pan in the oven and bake at 350° for 30 minutes.

NOTE: BE SURE TO USE HOT PADS WHEN YOU TAKE THE TOAST OUT OF THE OVEN. THE PAN WILL BE HOT.

6. Serve the French toast with sugar-free fruit topping.

Time to assemble: 10 minutes

Time to refrigerate: overnight

Time to bake: about 30 minutes

Makes 6 servings

Utensils:
9- by 13-inch baking pan, egg separator, measuring cup, measuring spoon, small bowl, whisk, plastic wrap, hot pads

PERFECT PANCAKES

Here's how to make great pancakes each and every time.

3 cups	Whole-wheat flour
1/2 cup	Dry buttermilk powder
1 tsp.	Baking soda
2 tsp.	Salt
2	Egg whites
3 cups	Milk (2%)
4 tsp.	Vegetable oil
	Vegetable oil cooking spray

1. In a large bowl, mix together the dry ingredients.

2. Use an egg separator to separate the yolks from the eggs. In a separate bowl, lightly beat the egg whites. Add the milk and the oil.

3. Pour the egg mixture into the flour mixture. Stir until all parts are wet. The batter will be kind of lumpy.

Utensils:
Measuring spoons, bowl, spoon, egg separator, frying pan, pancake turner, measuring cups

4. Spray a frying pan or griddle with vegetable oil cooking spray and heat the pan. You'll know it's hot enough when you drop a small drop of water on the surface and the water looks like it's dancing.

5. Use a 1/4-cup measure to dip into your pancake batter. Pour the batter onto the frying pan.

6. Cook each pancake until the top bubbles and the bubbles break. Then use a pancake turner and turn the pancakes over to brown the other side.

Serve these Perfect Pancakes with fresh fruit topping.

Time to assemble: 10 minutes

Time to cook: about 1 minute per pancake

Makes about 24 servings

Nutrition Information:

One serving	=	1 pancake
Calories	=	67
Fat	=	1 gm.
Carbohydrates	=	11 gm.
Protein	=	4 gm.
% Calories from fat	=	14%

SHAKE AND MAKE PANCAKES

Using a jar as your mixer instead of a bowl and spoon, you can shake yourself up a great breakfast.

1 1/3 cups	Milk (2%)
2	Egg whites
1 tsp.	Baking powder
1 Tbsp.	Vegetable oil
1 cup	Whole-wheat flour
	Vegetable oil cooking spray

1. Use an egg separator to separate the yolks from the egg whites. Set the egg whites aside.

2. Into a quart jar that has a screw-on lid, pour milk and egg whites. Screw the lid on the jar and shake until milk and eggs are thoroughly mixed.

3. Open the jar. Add baking powder and oil. Put the lid back on the jar and shake it again.

4. Open the jar. Spoon the whole wheat flour into the jar. Put the lid back on and shake the jar until the flour is thoroughly mixed with the milk. Set the jar aside.

5. Spray the griddle or frying pan with vegetable oil cooking spray and heat it on the stove over medium high heat.

Time to assemble: 10 minutes

Time to cook: about 1 minute per pancake

Makes 8 servingss

Utensils:
Egg separator, measuring cups, measuring spoons, 2-quart jar with lid, griddle or frying pan, pancake turner

6. When the pan or griddle is hot, pour the pancake batter onto the hot surface.

7. When bubbles form and break on the pancake, turn it over with a large pancake turner. Cook for about 1 minute.

8. Your pancakes are ready to serve. Decorate them with fresh fruit or paint them with the paint mix on the next page.

Nutrition Information:

One serving	=	1 pancake
Calories	=	92
Fat	=	2 gm.
Carbohydrates	=	13 gm.
Protein	=	4 gm.
% Calories from fat	=	22%

PAINT A PANCAKE

Here's a great excuse to play with your food. Make these toppings with different fruit juices and and store them separately in the refrigerator for when you want to use them. Get out your spoon and use it like a brush to paint your pancake or French toast.

2 cups	Fruit juice (Use one kind of juice for each recipe. Good choices are apple juice, grape juice, orange juice, or pineapple juice)
2 Tbsp.	Cornstarch (for each kind of juice)

1. Pour the fruit juice (only one kind) into a 1-quart saucepan and add the cornstarch. Use a whisk to mix the cornstarch with the fruit juice.

2. Put the saucepan on the stove and turn the stove on high. Use a long-handled wooden spoon to stir the mixture until is boils rapidly.

3. Turn off the stove. Remove the pan from the stove and your fruit topping is ready to serve. It will be hot, so be careful.

Time to assemble: 5 minutes

Time to cook: about 6 minutes

Each recipe makes 4 servings

Utensils:
1-quart saucepan, measuring cup, measuring spoon, whisk, long handled wooden spoon

Nutrition Information:

One serving	=	1/2 cup
Calories	=	41
Fat	=	0
Carbohydrates	=	10 gm.
Protein	=	0
% Calories from fat	=	0

THERE'S A MOUSE IN MY HOUSE PANCAKES

Here's another fun way to play with your food. Use the Shake and Make Pancake recipe and pour out the batter so it looks like Mickey Mouse. Decorate the mouse face with raisins, berries, cinnamon, or fruit slices. Have a contest with your family or friends to see who can create the best face.

You can try other shapes besides a mouse. How about trying to make a butterfly? Maybe a snowman? Use the Paint a Pancake recipe to make other creative toppings and have fun.

SPECIAL OCCASION SNACKS

When you are having your friends over for a party—your birthday or the last day of school—you can create some special snack foods that are fun to make.

PRETZELS

These are easy to make and great right out of the oven. Try spreading mustard on them.

1 Tbsp.	Yeast
1/2 cup	Warm water
1 tsp.	Honey
1 1/3 cups	Flour
1 tsp.	Salt
	Vegetable oil cooking spray

1. Preheat the oven to 325°.

2. Test your yeast by putting it in a measuring cup with the honey and the water. Stir. Part of the yeast will melt, part will stay in a lump. That's okay. Let the yeast sit for 5 minutes. It will be kind of bubbly and bigger than it was when you started. (If it isn't, your yeast has flunked the test and you need to start over with fresh yeast.)

Time to
assemble:
10 to 15
minutes

Time to bake:
10 minutes

Makes
12 servings

SPECIAL OCCASIONS

3. While the yeast is testing, measure the flour into a medium-sized bowl. Add the salt.

4. Add the yeast mixture to the flour mixture and stir it together. Start this with a spoon and finish it with your fingers.

5. While the dough is still flaky and crumbly put it on a cutting board that has a little flour sprinkled on it. Knead the dough, just like you would work with play-dough, until it forms a smooth ball.

6. Take a piece of dough about the size of a walnut and use your hands to roll it into a snake.

7. Shape the snake into a pretzel and put it on a cookie sheet sprayed with vegetable oil cooking spray. Keep doing this until you have used all the dough. You should have 12 pretzels.

8. Bake the pretzels for 10 minutes.

Utensils:
Measuring cup, measuring spoons, wooden spoon, medium-sized bowl, cutting board, cookie sheet, hot pads

Nutrition Information:

One serving	=	1 pretzel
Calories	=	53
Fat	=	1 gm.
Carbohydrates	=	11 gm.
Protein	=	2 gm.
% Calories from fat	=	3%

TORTILLA CHIPS WITH HOMEMADE SALSA

Feel like making something Mexican? Try this.

8   Corn tortillas (Thinner is better. They are sometimes known as table tortillas.)
Vegetable oil cooking spray
Water in a spray bottle
Salt

1. Preheat oven to 350°.

2. Cut each tortilla into 4 pieces by cutting in half and then cutting each half again. The pieces are shaped like pie pieces.

3. Spray a cookie sheet with vegetable oil cooking spray.

4. Layer tortillas on the cookie sheet without overlapping.

Utensils:
Knife, cutting board, cookie sheet, spray bottle, hot pads

5. Spray tortillas with water.

6. Sprinkle tortillas with salt.

7. Bake for about 15 minutes. They should be crisp, but not dark.

8. When the tortillas are cool, store them in tightly sealed plastic bags. As you close the bag, press as much of the air out as you can.

Nutrition Information:

One serving	=	6 chips
Calories	=	58
Fat	=	1 gm.
Carbohydrates	=	12 gm.
Protein	=	1 gm.
% Calories from fat	=	6%

Time to assemble: 5 minutes

Time to bake: 15 minutes

Makes 32 chips

SALSA

2	Ripe tomatoes (or you can use a 14 1/2-oz. can of diced tomatoes)
1/2 cup	Chopped onion
1 tsp.	Cilantro, minced
1/4 tsp.	Salt
1/4 cup	Water
4 1/2-oz. can	Mild chili peppers, chopped

1. Chop the tomatoes and put them in a medium bowl.

2. Chop the onion and add it to the tomatoes.

3. Use a scissors to snip the cilantro into small pieces. Add it to the mix.

Utensils:
Knife, cutting board, medium bowl, measuring cup, measuring spoons, can opener, scissors

4. Add salt and water.

5. Add peppers to the salsa one spoonful at a time. Stir and taste after you add each spoonful. Stop adding peppers when it tastes the way you like it.

6. Serve with your homemade tortilla chips.

Nutrition Information:

One serving	=	1/2 cup
Calories	=	26
Fat	=	trace
Carbohydrates	=	5 gm.
Protein	=	1 gm.
% Calories from fat	=	7%

Time to assemble: 15 minutes

Makes 5 servings

LET'S TRY A PIE

Making a pie can be fun when you have some time to spend in the kitchen. This recipe is great for special occasions.

2 cups	Milk (2%), each cup in its own cup
1 3-oz. pkg.	Sugar-free chocolate pudding (not instant)
1 9-inch	Prepared graham cracker pie crust
1 3-oz. pkg.	Sugar-free vanilla pudding (not instant)
4 large	Bananas

1. Pour 1 cup of milk and the chocolate pudding mix into a medium saucepan.

2. Cook over medium high heat until the pudding is thick.

3. Pour the pudding into the pie crust.

4. Wash the saucepan out and pour in the other cup of milk. Add the vanilla pudding mix.

5. Cook it over medium high heat until it is thick.

Utensils:
Medium saucepan,
stirring spoon,
measuring cups,
knife

6. Peel and slice the bananas, then place them on top of the chocolate pudding layer. Pour the vanilla pudding over the top of the bananas.

7. Refrigerate the pie for 2 hours.

Note: You can decorate the top of your pie with a little bit of hard chocolate. Use a vegetable peeler to make some thin slices of chocolate. They should curl. Put the curled chocolate on the top of the pie. (Something that decorates food is called a "garnish.")

Nutrition Information:

One serving	=	1/8 pie
Calories	=	151
Fat	=	3 gm.
Carbohydrates	=	29 gm.
Protein	=	2 gm.
% Calories from fat	=	18%

Time to assemble: 15 minutes

Time to refrigerate: 2 hours

Makes 8 servings

PURPLE MOO MOO

When you are in charge of making the drinks, here's a really special one.

2 cups	Purple grape juice
1 cup	Nonfat frozen vanilla yogurt

1. Combine the grape juice and frozen yogurt in the blender.

2. Blend until the mixture is smooth.

3. Pour into 4 glasses and serve.

Time to assemble: 5 minutes

Makes 4 servings

Utensils:
Electric blender,
measuring cups,
4 glasses

Nutrition Information:

One serving	=	2/3 cup
Calories	=	156
Fat	=	0
Carbohydrates	=	37 gm.
Protein	=	2 gm.
% Calories from fat	=	0

SPECIAL OCCASIONS

Icy Pops

This is just for fun.

1 12-oz. can	Frozen Cran-Raspberry® juice concentrate
2 cups	Water

1. Combine the juice concentrate with the water in a pitcher.
2. Pour into 8 small paper cups.
3. Insert a Popsicle® stick into each cup.
4. Freeze until firm.

Time to assemble: 10 minutes

Time to freeze: 2 hours

Makes 8 servings

Utensils:
Pitcher,
measuring cup,
paper cups,
Popsicle® sticks

Nutrition Information:

One serving	=	1 pop cup
Calories	=	66
Fat	=	0
Carbohydrates	=	16 gm.
Protein	=	0
% Calories from fat	=	0

SPECIAL OCCASIONS

INDEX

A

Abbreviations, 28
About vitamins and minerals, 4
After-School Applesauce, 92
After-school snacks, 87-109
Aloha Flip, 150
Alphaghetti, 116
Apple Crisp, 146
Applesauce, 39, 92
Apples, Cinnamon, 105

B

Bake-It-Yourself Banana Bread, 160
Baked goods, 153-161
Baked Potatoes, 97
Baked Tomatoes, 134
Banana Blitz, 35
Banana Bread, 80, 160
Banana on a Stick, 38
Bananarama Muffins, 158
Basic French Dressing, 138
Basic Spaghetti with Meatless Sauce, 112
Beetle Muffins, 156
Blender Applesauce, 39
Blender Banana Blitz, 35
Body temperature, 5
Breakfast Granola Bars, 48
Breakfast recipes, 32-55
Breakfast, why eat, 31

Brownies, 84
Brunch Recipes, 162-173
Butter Buds®, 16
Buttermilk Dressing, 137

C

Calcium, 4
Calories, about, 9
Carbohydrates, 2, 10
Carrot Cut-Ups, 96
Cereal Mix, 106
Cheesy Chicken Sandwiches, 68
Cheesy Green Beans, 136
Cherry Soup, 40
Chicken Dishes, 120-125
Chicken Nuggets, 120
Chili, Kids' Quick, 60
Chilly Cherry Soup, 40
Chinese Stir-fry with Shrimp, 130
Chocolate Chippies, 82
Choosing to eat healthy stuff, 1
Cinnamon Apples for Four, 105
Cleanup, 30
Colorful Coleslaw, 64
Cooking directions, 25-27
Cooking terms, 25-28
Cornbread, Southern, 78
Cory's Crunchy Crust Pizza, 75
Creamy Scrambled Eggs, 50
Creamy Tuna on Toast, 128
Crunchy Cereal Mix, 106
Cucumber Circles, 94

D

Dairy foods, 3
Desserts, 82-85, 146-152
Dinner, 111-152
Dippity Dilly Vegetable Dip, 73
Dressings, 137-141

E

Easy Lasagna, 118
Eating when Hungry, 105
Eggs-Citing Surprise, 52
Eggs, Scrambled, 50
Evening Meal, 111
Equivalents, 29
EZ Orange Sherbet, 152

F

Fast food for lunch ideas, 58
Fats, 2, 10
Fish Dishes, 126-131
Fish in a Flash, 126
Fizzy Fruit Slush, 36
Flip, Aloha, 150
Food Guide Pyramid, 2,4
Food groups, 2
French Toast, 162, 166
Friendly Fowl in Foil Chicken
    Dinner Bake, 124
Fruit Fling, 34
Fruit Flurry, 91
Fruit for lunch, 70

Fruit Kabobs, 88
Fun with Lunches, 57

G

Gingerbread Muffin Mix, 154
Grams, 10
Granola 45, 46, 48
Grapes, Icy, 44
Green Beans, 136

H

Homemade Granola, 45
How to measure food, 6
How to read labels, 10

I

Icy Grapes to Go, 44
Icy Pops, 183

K

Kabobs, 88
Katie's Paint Your Pizza, 102
Kids' Quick Chili, 60
Kitchen safety, 16-17
Kitchen tools, 18-24

L

Labels, 10-11
Lasagna, 118
Lazy-Day Choices, 49

Learn the pyramid, 3

Lunch ideas and recipes, 57-85

M

Magnesium, 4

Main Dishes, 111-152

Make-A-Face Breakfast
  Sandwiches, 53

Meatballs, 114

Measuring, 6, 8, 10

Mighty Fine French Toast, 162

Mighty Fine Fudge Brownies, 84

Minerals, 2, 4

Mini Veggie Pizza, 76

Molly McButter®, 16

Muffins,
  Bananarama, 158
  Beetle, 156
  Gingerbread, 154

N

Nuggets, Chicken, 120

Nutrients, 2

Nutrition Facts, 10

Nutrition, 9

O

On-the-Bus Breakfasts, 49

Open-faced Pizzawich, 104

P

Paint a Pancake, 172

Painted Toast, 51

Pancakes, 168, 170

Perfect Pops, 90

Pickety Pockety, 69

Pie, Let's Try, 180

Pizza, 75, 76, 102, 104

Pocketful of Tuna, 67

Potato Chips, Sweet, 74

Potato Salad, 132

Potato Wedgies, 100

Potatoes, Baked, 97

Pretzels, 174

Protein, 2, 3, 10

Purple Moo Moo, 182

R

Radish Flowers, 95

Raspberry Smoothie, 33

Reading labels, 10

Really Nice Chicken with Rice, 122

Rice Puff Fluff, 43

S

Safety, 16

Salad Dressings, 137-145

Salads, 62-66, 137

Salsa, 178

Sandwiches, 53, 67-69, 102-104

Scrambled Eggs, 50

Selenium, 4

Serving sizes, 8

Shake and Make Pancakes, 170

Sherbet, 152

Shrimp, Stir-Fry, 130

Side-Dish Broiled Meatballs, 114

Slush, 36

Smoothie, Raspberry, 33

Snacks 87-110, 173

Snowy Fruit Flurry, 90

Sodium, 11

Sorry Charlie Sailboats, 103

Southern Cornbread, 78

Spaghetti, Basic, 112

Special snacks, 173-183

Strawberry Dressing, 140

Sunny Days Salad, 72

Sunny Honey Banana Bread, 80

Sunshine Salad, 70

Super Snack Bars, 108

Sweet and Chunky Toast Topper, 164

Sweet Potato Chips, 74

T

Tangy Taters, 54

Tater Toppers, 98

There's a Mouse in My House
  Pancakes, 173

Three Fruit Salad, 142

Toast, Painted, 51

Toast, Topper, 164

Tools, 18

Tortilla Chips with Homemade
  Salsa, 176

Tossed Super Salad, 66

Tunapple Salad with Orange
  Dressing, 62

Tuna on Toast, 128

Tuna Sailboats, 103

U

Understanding calories, 9

V

Veggie Kabobs, 88

Vitamins, 2, 4

W

Water, about, 5

What's in a good meal? 2

Wobbly Fruit, 148

Words to help you, 25

Y

Yokota Salad, 144

Yogurt, 90, 182